TABLE OF CONTENTS

Introduction ii

Section One: Communication Tools and Layout Design 1

Graphic Devices 2

Using Borders, Boxes, and Rules 4

Styles of Drop/Initial Caps 6

Use of Drop/Initial Caps 8

Using Graphic Devices Consistently 10

Balance 11

Visual Syntax 12

Cultural Sensitivity 13

The Obvious "Z" 14

Connecting Copy to Action 16

Implied Motion 18

Getting Full-Page Effect at Half Price 20

The Arithmetic Sequence 21

Highlighting One Image 23

Adapting Good Ideas 24

Change Only for a Good Reason 25

The Scholar's Margin Grid 28

Tables of Contents 29

Complex Grids 31

Section Two: Text Design 34

Readability 35

Beware of Text Set Ragged Left 37

Text Can Control Syntax 39

Design for Your Objective 40

Some Good Ideas Don't Work 41

Two Fonts Are Plenty 43

Matching the Text Design to the Audience 44

Enhancing Legibility With Two-Weight Serif Fonts . . . 45

Maintaining Legibility 46

Sharp Contrast Is Eye-Catching 47

Surprinting Text on Art 48

Copy-Heavy Doesn't Mean Copy-Dense 49

Section Three: Creativity in Design 50

Tilting to Convey a Feeling of Liveliness 51

Vertical Layouts Unify Documents 53

Connecting Ideas With a Mortice 55

Using Borders to Send Messages 56

Getting Attention or Creating a Mood With Type . . 62

Messages in Frame Layouts Get Read 66

The Mondrian Layout 68

Unusual Shapes Carry Clout 70

A Rebus 73

One Piece of Content: Five Different Looks 75

Glossary 80

Bibliography 84

References 85

Acknowledgments 87

About the Author 88

INTRODUCTION

Step by step, from setting your design objectives to executing professional-quality designs, this book will show you the way.

In the following pages, design themes are developed and fully explained. You'll learn the basics of design theory — research-based and comprehensive, detailed in straightforward and easy-to-understand language.

You'll be able to use these tried-and-true design shortcuts now and for years to come. The approaches discussed here work, and they're adaptable for your needs. You'll refer to the examples over and over again as you make them your own. By looking at samples from a variety of media, you'll be able to see how effective design isn't media-specific; that is, just because a featured example is an ad, it doesn't mean that the idea can't be adapted to a brochure, a flyer, a proposal, or a catalog.

In order to understand and use this book, you need to be familiar with various definitions and conventions. The glossary defines key design terms and explains how they're commonly used among professionals. The first time we reference a key term it will be set in **boldface** — when you see a word set in bold, flip to the glossary and familiarize yourself with the definition.

To use this book, you don't need either a design background or a specific desktop publishing program ... in fact, even if you're designing using an exacto knife and masking film, this book will help you. It's a book about design, not about computers. Tips, shortcuts, and potential pitfalls specific to desktop publishing are discussed, and the design ideas detailed here are easily applicable to the desktop environment.

This book is divided into three sections. You'll follow the design process from concept to execution.

Section One covers Communication Tools and Layout Design. You'll learn which tools are available, what they do, and how to use them to lay out the page for maximum effectiveness.

Section Two discusses Text Design. The decisions you make about type are key to your design's success; no matter what your primary objective is, you always have at least a secondary objective to have your material read. You'll learn the rules of readability, the powerful way type can convey specific images, and how to determine when to break the rules.

Section Three reviews the role of creativity in design. Design shortcuts are explained so that you'll understand how to apply them to your projects.

Throughout the book, the examples reinforce the three guiding principles of effective design:

- You must have a clear understanding of your objective, that objective must be narrowly defined, and it must have an action orientation.

- You must target a specific audience and know enough about your readers to understand how to reach them. It doesn't matter that you may be attracted to a certain design; what matters is whether that design is likely to work.

- It all starts with an idea. Without a concept, designs look disorganized, disharmonious, and amateurish. Without a concept, success is accidental. And it doesn't need to be.

Follow along and you'll discover how to take these three principles — what you know about your readers, what you want to accomplish, and a focused concept — and meld them into an effective, successful design every time.

Jane K. Cleland

HOW TO CREATE HIGH-IMPACT DESIGNS

SECTION ONE: COMMUNICATION TOOLS AND LAYOUT DESIGN

In this section, we'll review the tools available to you in your efforts to communicate in print, and we'll go over which tools make sense to use in which applications. This first set of examples will display specific design tools, explain how readers read, demonstrate various ways of controlling syntax, and help ensure your designs are clear and your emphasis is correct. With a solid base in these fundamental communication devices, you'll be able to spot weak areas in your designs — and you'll know how to correct them. You'll also get insight into which tools draw a reader's eye, making your layouts compelling and effective.

GRAPHIC DEVICES

Graphic devices accomplish two things. First, they encourage readers to perceive reading as non-threatening and nonintimidating; second, they quickly and easily communicate a specific concept, idea, or attitude.

Graphic devices are symbols — things that are understood to have a certain meaning, or that convey information because of a culture's shared understanding.

As soon as you see these symbols (below and at right), you know exactly what is represented ... quotation marks and an exclamation mark. So do your readers. In our society, these symbols — examples of graphic devices — are easily and quickly understood. Graphic devices are very powerful ways to swiftly convey a great deal of information among people who share an understanding of the symbols.

Consider the quotation marks.

On one level, they simply signal that what's contained inside are the exact words of the speaker. But there's a deeper understanding. Your readers are likely to perceive that what's contained within the marks is "conversational," and therefore they'll expect it to be livelier — and more interesting — than the same number of words set in narrative would be. Your reader will also perceive copy set in quotes as shorter.

Bottom line: Copy set in quotes is more likely to be read than the same number of words set in a traditional narrative style.

The exclamation point serves a similar purpose: Readers understand that if there's an exclamation point, there's something exciting going on. And that helps motivate them to read it. That's true whether the exclamation point is used as a typographic symbol or as a design element.

The dotted line is another good example of the power of shared cultural understanding. All that's here is a dotted line going in four directions, but your readers understand an entire set of instructions from it. They understand that they're to cut it out, fill it in, and mail it off. Think about that! All that information conveyed by a dotted line.

When we add the **clip-art** scissors, we're sending two graphic signals ... we're saying, "We mean it! Cut this out!"

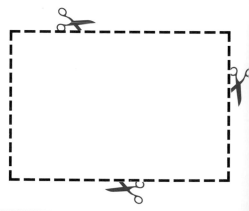

Call-outs also can help make technical material seem less intimidating. By using call-outs, you can enable your readers to approach technical information in bite-size pieces. They'll be much more likely to approach your document if it looks as if they can do so at their own pace. Call-outs help convey this perception.

Notice in this next example how effective the call-outs are. It isn't just the use of the rule and arrowhead, of course. Note that the names are treated as headlines — they're bigger and bolder than the rest. The **em dash** separates the heading from the text. Isn't it more likely this small amount of text will be read than if we'd set it as a four- or five-line caption?

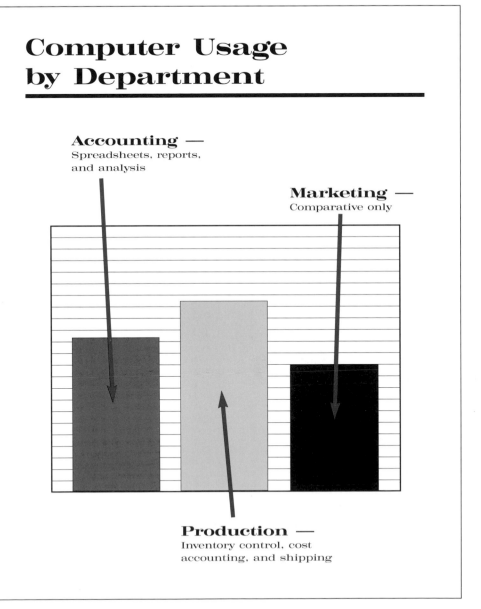

Computer Usage by Department

Accounting —
Spreadsheets, reports, and analysis

Marketing —
Comparative only

Production —
Inventory control, cost accounting, and shipping

Use call-outs when you have a few key points you want to highlight. By breaking large chunks of copy into bite-size pieces, you make it much more likely that your readers will get your message.

USING BORDERS, BOXES, AND RULES

Rules can also contribute to a finished look, adding definition. You can use rules as borders, boxes, and call-outs. In this example, note how **keylining** helps the photograph look "framed." Adding a few points of **white space** adds polish.

By keylining the photo, we're accomplishing two things: We're achieving that "finished" look, and we're creating a sense of perspective, a feeling of depth, of stepping into the scenery.

Rules, boxes, and borders serve to separate one section of a layout from another, or to connect one section to another.

*P*icture yourself relaxing
in beautiful
*A*rizona

You'll hike in these
spectacular mountains

This refreshing
pool awaits!

Wave "hi!" to your
friends back home!

Go West Travel

Note the arrows in the Arizona example. Notice how they encourage reading the three key selling points ... and how they direct the eye into the photographs which support and enhance the call-out copy.

One technique to help you achieve this harmonious marriage of text and **art** in your brochures is to work with your copywriter before the photographs are taken. Write the captions and call-outs first. You can then instruct the photographer to take the shot described in the caption or call-out.

STYLES OF DROP/INITIAL CAPS

Drop — or initial (inish) — caps can be hand drawn or designed in your desktop publishing system. A staff or freelance artist can draw 26 letters just for you. These letters featuring animals would be appropriate for a variety of organizations including a zoo, a pet store, or a college of veterinary science, for example. By scanning them into the system, you'd have them available for a variety of applications.

Another option is simply enlarging the fonts you've selected and are already using. Either your headline or body text font can be used effectively. This simple alternative is appropriate only for layouts where lively graphics would be suitable.

One doesn't need to be an artist or have a huge budget to create effective drop caps. These six drop caps were all executed in Adobe Illustrator. As you look at them, you can see that simplicity enhances design.

Note the double line above the letter A; this concept is repeated in the outline font of the A itself. The strong, angular simplicity would be a good choice for a company looking for an image of precision and strength — say a scientific testing facility, for example.

The M is enhanced by a clip-art vine. The letter remains legible, but the delicate vine implies dignity or elegance. How about using this style for an upscale garden center trying to convey an image of refined service? Or an outdoor cafe?

The E is **knocked out** of a black box. Texture was added to the white area. You can scan in your own textures, or use standard ones available in Illustrator and other programs. (For example, try scanning in crumpled-up aluminum foil, sandpaper, ceramic tiles, or wicker.) This looks modern and fun ... can you see how it might be appropriate for a rock 'n' roll radio station, a trendy men's clothing store, or a software consulting company? Texture adds variety and distinction, and if you scan in your own texture, you can create a look that's unique to you.

The K is positioned in a diamond shape. Note how the wavy background creates a feeling of motion, energy, or water; and how the keyline contributes to a sense of depth. This design might work for a spa and pool company or a public relations firm.

Note that the drop shadow on the Y takes a simple letter and adds a bit of polish. The curves of the letter add to the informal, relaxed feel. This might work for a day care center or a party supply store.

The outline script W is on a **screened** background in an elliptical shape that has been keylined. The script creates a formal or feminine feel; the elliptical shape carries through the "softer" image. How about this style of drop cap for a woman's clothing store or a caterer?

USE OF DROP/INITIAL CAPS

Use drop or inish caps only to signal a significant beginning. For example, it's appropriate to use a drop cap at the beginning of each chapter, but not each paragraph.

Following the principle of simplicity, it would be preferable to use a drop cap only at the start of the master article in a newsletter, not every article; at the beginning of each section of a proposal, not every subsection; and at the start of a company's brochure, not at the start of each panel.

Note how confusing the proliferation of drop caps is in the first example. It just looks silly. Readers stare, bewildered, trying to apply logic: Is there a secret sentence here?

Because drop/inish caps send a signal of a beginning, they're a terrific tool to use when you want your reader to scan your material. But as this example shows, their overuse defeats the purpose; one doesn't know where to "enter" the copy, and thus won't read it at all.

Drop/inish caps should be sized at about three to six times body copy size. Note that when they're too large, they overwhelm the design. The columns are too narrow, and readers try to start each sentence with the large letter.

Also notice how the art — which is attractive, appropriate, and harmonious with the concept, fades away.

It can't compete with the overpowering drop caps. Contrast the two Franklin Furniture examples (on this page and the next). With the drop caps sized properly, the design is enhanced.

Desktop Publishing
Allow Your Imagination Free Rein

Lorem ipsum dolor sit amet, consectetuer adipiscing elit. Ased diam nonummy nibh euismod tincidunt ut laoreet dolore aliquam erat. Ut wisi enim ad minim veniam, quis nostrud exerci tation ullam. Corper suscipit lobortis nisl ut aliquip ex ea commodo consequat. Duis autem vel eum iriure dolor in hendrerit in vulputate. Velit esse molestie consequat, vel illum dolore eu feugiat nulla faisis. Eat vero eros et accumsan froat iusto odio dignissim quirie blandit praesent luptat.Buis autem vel eum iriure dolor in. Hendrerit in vulputate velit esse moleste. Scouat, vel illum dolore eu feugiat nulla facilisis at. Wiusto odio dignissim qui blandit

prusent. Oluptatum zzril delenit augue duis dolore te feugait nulla facilisi. At wisi enim ad veniam, quis nostrud exerci tation ullamcorper suscipit lobortis. Nis ut aliquip ex ea com. Lorem ipsum dolor sit amet, consectetuer. Tek piscing elit, sed diam nonummy nibh euismod tinsi. utpat. Etes wisi enim ad minim veniam, quis nostrud exerci tation uamcorper. Rucipit lobortis nisl ut aliquip ex ea omep. Sorem ipsum dolor sit amet, consectetuer Yadipiscing elit, sed diam nonuy nibh Uismod tinsi. Lorem ipsum dolor sit amet. Donsectetuer adcing elit. Sed diam nonummy ibh euismod. Vincidunt trut laoreet dolorem. Agna

Zuis autem vel eum iriure dolor in hendrerit in vulputate velit. Fesse molestie consquat, vel illum dolore eu feugiat nula facilis at vero. Jeros et accumsan et iusto odio. Nissim.Suis san froat iusto odio autem vel eum iri-dignissim quirie blan-ure dolor in hendr-dit praesent luptat.Buis rit in. Nulputate autem vel eum iriure velit esse molestie dolor. Froat iusto odio consequat, velper. dignissim. Tillum dolore eu feugiat nulla facilisis at vero eros set. accumsan. Et en iusto odio dissim. blandit paesent. utpat.

At Franklin Furniture, Fabrics Are Foremost

Suis autem vel eum iriure dolor in hendrerit in vulputate velit esse molestie consequat, vel illum dolore eu feugiat nulla facilisis at vero eros et accumsan et iusto odio dignissim qui blandit praesent luptatum zzril delenit augue duis dolore te feugait nulla. Lorem ipsum dolor sit amet, consectetuer adipiscing elit, sed diam nonummy nibh euismod tinsi. Lorem ipsum dolor sit amet, consectetuer adipiscing elit, sedfacilisis at vero eros et accumsan et iusto odio dignissim qui blandit. Praesent luptatum zzril delenit augue duis dolore te feugait nulla facilisi. Lorem ipsum dolor sit amet, consectetuer adipiscing elit, sed.

Diam nonummy nibh euismod tinsi. Lorem ipsum dolor sit ameti. Lorem ipsu facilisis at vero eros et accumsan et iusto odio dignissim qui blandit praesent luptatum zzril delenit augue duis dolore te feugait nulla facilisi. Lorem ipsum.

Buis autem vel eum iriure dolor in hendrerit in vulputate velit esse illum dolore eu feugiat nulla facilisis at vero eros et accumsan et iusto odio dignissim qui blandit praesent luptatum zzril delenit augue duis dolore te feugait nulla faciuis

Kuis autem vel eum iriure dolor in hendrerit in vulputate velit esse mole stie consequat, vel ill autem vel eum iriure dolor in hendrerit in vulputate velit esse molestie conseAnsectetuer adipiscing elity nibh euismod tinsi. Lorem ipsum facilisis at vero eros et.

Get iusto odio dignissim qui blandit praesent luptatum zzril delenit augue duis t, consectetuer adipiscing elit, sed diam.

At Franklin Furniture, Fabrics Are Foremost

Suis autem vel eum iriure dolor in hendrerit in vulputate velit esse molestie consequat, vel illum dolore eu feugiat nulla facilisis at vero eros et accumsan et iusto odio dignissim.

Dui blandit praesent luptatum zzril delenit augue duis dolore te feugait nulla facilisi. Lorem ipsum dolor sit amet, consectetuer adipiscing elit, sed diam nonummy nibh euismod tinsi. Lorem ipsum dolor sit amet, consectetuer adipiscing elit, sedfacilisis at vero eros et accumsan et iusto odio dignissim qui blandit. Praesent luptatum zzril delenit augue duis dolore te feugait nulla facilisi.

Lorem ipsum dolor sit amet, consectetuer adipiscing elit.

Diam nonummy nibh euismod tinsi. Lorem ipsum dolor

sit amet, consectetuer adipiscing elit, sed diam nonummy nibh euismod tinsi. Lorem ipsum dolor sit ameti.

Buis autem vel eum iriure dolor in hendrerit in vulputate velit esse illum dolore eu feugiat nulla facilisis at vero eros.

Accumsan et iusto odio dignissim qui blandit praesent luptatum zzril delenit augue duis dolore te feugait nulla faciuis.

Wllum dolore eu feugiat nulla facilisis at vero eros kdog dospclip.

Accumsan et iusto odio dignissim qui blandit praesent luptatum zzril delenit augue duis dolore te feugait nulla faciuis sent luptatum zzril delenit augue duis dolore te feugait nu.

Lorem ipsu facilisis at vero eros et accumsan et iusto odio dignissim qui blandit praesent luptatum zzril delenit augue duis dolore te feugait nulla facilisi gorem ripsum.

Dui blandit praesent luptatum zzril delenit augue duis

dolore te feugait nulla facilisi. Lorem ipsum dolor sit amet, consectetuer adipiscing elit, sed diam nonummy nibh euismod tinsi.

Kuis autem vel eum iriure dolor in hendrerit in vulputate velit esse molestie consequat, vel ill autem vel eum iriure dolor in hendrerit in vulputate velit esse olestie conse. Ansectetuer adipiscing elity nibh euismod tinsi. Lorem ipsum facilisis at vero eros et.

Get iusto odio dignissim qui blandit praesent luptatum zzril delenit augue duis, consectetuer adipiscing elit, sed diam.

Also notice how the initial cap **font** picks up the style of art used in the chairs, and matches (but doesn't replicate) the headline font. It is the weight that's varied, not the style.

Maintaining a consistent "feel" always adds to a design's appeal and the publishing organization's professionalism.

USING GRAPHIC DEVICES CONSISTENTLY

!dea Source uses a variety of tools to create its image. By replacing the letter "I" with an exclamation point, the concept of excitement is connected to the name — and through the name to the entire newsletter, thus dramatically enhancing its perceived value. Notice how the use of a dot picks up the power of the exclamation point and is continued throughout the layout in the border, bullet points, and the coupon.

Icons signal that one section of the layout is different from another, and provide an indication of the content of each section. Note how the leaf crosses the **grid** line, adding a sense of depth. The text wraps just a bit so **readability** isn't an issue.

!DEA SOURCE

Travel Strategy

Lorem ipsum dolor sit amet, consectetuer adipiscing elit, sed diam nonummy nibh euismod tinsi. Lorem ipsum dolor sit amet, consectetuer adipiscing elit, sedfacilisis at vero eros et accumsan et iusto odio dignissim.

Praesent luptatum zzril delenit augue duis dolore te feugait nulla facilisi. Lorem ipsum dolor sit amet, consectetuer adipiscing Diam nonummy nibh euismod tinsi. Lorem ipsum dolor sit ameti.Lorem ipsu facilisis at vero eros et accumsan et iusto odio dignissim qui blandit praesent luptatum zzril delenit augue duis dolore te feugait nulla facilisi. Lorem ipsum. sedfacilisis at vero eros et accumsan et iusto odio dignissim qui blandit. sedfacilisis at vero eros et accumsan et iusto odio dignissim qui blan

Lorem ipsum dolor sit amet, consectetuer adipiscing elit, sed diam nonummy nibh euismod tinsi. Lorem ipsum dolor sit amet, consectetuer adipiscing elit, sedfacilisis at vero eros et accumsan et iusto odion.

Diam nonummy nibh euismod tinsi. Lorem ipsum dolor sit ameti.Lorem ipsu facilisis at vero eros et accumsan et iusto odio dignissim qui blandit praesent luptatum zzril delenit augue duis dolore te feugait null. ●

Career Moves

Wedfacilisis at vero eros et accumsan et iusto odio dignissim qui blandit. sedfacilisis at vero eros et accumsan et iusto

odio dignissim qui blandit. Dfeugait nulla facilisi. Lorem ipsum. sedfacilisis at vero eros et a. feugait nulla facilisi. Lorem ipsum. sedfacilisis at vero ero. Rfeugait nulla facilisi. Lorem ipsum. sedfacilisis at vero eros ten. nissim qui blandit praesent luptatum zzril delenit augue duis dolore te feugait nulla facilisi. Lorem ipsum. sedfacilisis at.. blandit. sedfacilisis at vero eros et accumsan et iusto odio dignissim qui blandit. Dfeugait nulla facilisi. Lorem ipsum. sedfacilisis at. Ggait nulla facilisi. Lorem ipsum. sedfacili.blandit. sedfacilisis at vero eros et acums. ●

Getting Back to Nature

Fodio tdignis sim qui blandit. Dfeugait nulla facilisi. Lorem ipsum. sedfacilisis at vero eros et a. feugait nulla facilisi. Lorem ipsum sit amet, consect.

Lorem ipsum dolor sit amet, consectetuer adipiscing elit, sed diam nonummy nibh euismod tinsi. Lorem ipsum dolor sit amet, consectetuer adipiscing elit, sedfacilisis at vero eros et accumsan et iusto odio dignissim qui blandit.

Praesent luptatum zzril delenit augue duis dolore te feugait nulla facilisi. Lorem ipsum dolor sit amet, consectetuer adipiscing Diam nonummy nibh euismod tinsi. Lorem ipsum dolor sit ameti.Lorem ipsu facilisis at vero eros et accumsan et iusto odio dignissim qui blandit praesent luptatum zzril delenit augue duis dolore te feugait nulla facilisi. Lorem ipsum. sedfacilisis at vero eros et accumsan et iusto odio dignissim qui blandit. sedfacilisis.

Lorem ipsum dolor sit amet, consectetuer adipisci, mod tinsi. Lorem ipsum dolor sit amet, consectetuer adipiscing elit, sedfacilisis at vero eros et accumsan et iusto odio dignissim. ●

Postal Victories

Praesent luptatum zzril delenit augue duis dolore te feugait nulla facilisi. Lorem ipsum. sedfacilisis at vero eros et accumsan et iusto odio dignissim qui blandit. sedfacilisis at vero eros et accumsan et iusto odio dignissim qui blandit. Dfeugait nulla facilisi. Lorem ipsum. sedfacilisis at vero eros et a. feugait nulla facilisi. Lorem ipsum. sedfacilisis at vero ero. Rfeugait nulla facilisi. Lorem ipsum. sedfacilisis at vero eros ten. nissim qui blandit praesent luptatum zzril delenit augue duis dolore te feugait nulla facilisi. Lorem ipsum. sedfacilisis at.. blandit. sedfacilisis at vero eros et accumsan et iusto odio dignissim qui blandit. Dfeugait nulla facilisi. Lorem ipsum. sedfacilisis at. Ggait nulla facilisi, Lorem ipsum sedfacili.blandit. sedfacilisis at vero eros et accumsan et iusto odio dignissim qui blandit. Lorem feugait nulla facilisi. Lorem ipsum sedfacil. ●

Great !dea! I want a subscription to !DEA SOURCE.

Name: _____

Address: _____

ski: _____

mirt: _____

Deugait nulla facilisi. Lorem ipsum. sedfacilisis at. Ggait nulla facilisi, Lorem ipsum sedfacili.blandit.

BALANCE

Maintaining balance is a foundational concept of layout design.

There are two ways to achieve balance: symmetrically and asymmetrically. Most designers prefer asymmetry, as it's more visually interesting. But remember there's nothing inherently wrong with symmetry. And it's often easier to design a symmetrical layout.

Understanding what contributes to a pleasing sense of balance makes it easy to achieve. There are six rules of balance:

1 Anything located in the upper left quadrant (the **primary optical area**) of a layout is more heavily weighted than anything located anywhere else.

2 Large items are noticed more, seen for a longer time, and remembered better than are small items.

3 **Elements** that are dark carry more **optical weight** than elements that are light.

4 Color conveys more optical weight than black and white.

Consider what this means: An element that meets the following standards (on any size layout) is extremely powerful. If it's:

- Dark in tone or hue,

- In color (four color or spot color),

- Larger than other elements on the layout, and

- Positioned in the upper left-hand quadrant — it will be noticed.

One can **counterbalance** this powerful element with:

5 White space. It serves to draw readers' attention to whatever is in the "non-empty" space.

6 Rectangles (except for perfect squares) are usual shapes. Everything else conveys optical weight. This means triangles, ovals, circles, elliptical shapes, cubes, and others all convey optical weight.

You'll see many examples of the principle of balance throughout this book.

Primary optical area

Balance means right equals left, and top equals bottom. If the layout is out of balance, it looks jarring. Worst of all, the most important elements may go unnoticed.

VISUAL SYNTAX

The "Z" path is considered the normal eye path.

The five areas highlighted here show the "normal" viewing pattern. Readers' eyes start slightly to the left and above center, move up a bit, then to the right, down on the diagonal, and then right to the **terminal area.**

If you connect the "dots," the areas of attention describe the letter "Z." The "Z" path is considered the normal eye path.

Lay your elements down according to the "Z," or do something else to direct your readers' eyes in an appropriate sequence. In other words, control the **syntax.** It's critical that you're able to predict what your reader sees first, what they see second, and so on.

Just as your company's best salespeople know what to say first, when to make various points, and how to lead the sales presentation to the "close" or action step, so too should you, as the designer, control the presentation of information. No matter what your objective — whether it's overtly sales-oriented or not — controlling the syntax is key to success. And that means you need to know how your readers read. If they read the way we do, the "Z" path is appropriate.

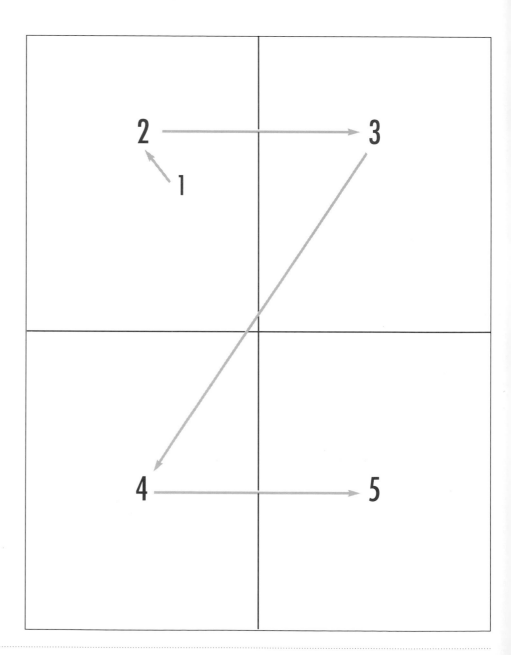

CULTURAL SENSITIVITY

The issue of cultural sensitivity is critical because not all readers read the way we read. Consider this example of a product spec sheet. Notice the syntax that's been created is the top half of the "Z" path. We start with an unpleasant-looking, sick person with an upset stomach, move logically — from left to right — to the product, Magnex Antacid, and finally, end up with a happy, better-feeling person. Magnex Antacid gets results!

While the "Z" path is considered normal for those who read the way we do, many, many cultures do *not* read our way. Be careful that the syntax you create is appropriate for your target audience.

This is especially important if you are designing multilanguage publications. Many Asian cultures, for instance, read top to bottom. So if you have a brochure targeting both readers of a

to translate and design them individually. A common concern in situations such as this is that you lose the harmony of a piece by creating different syntaxes. However, by using the same graphic devices, fonts, size, color, and the like, a sense of unity will be maintained, while independent syntaxes are created.

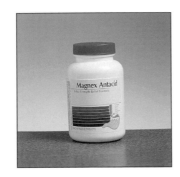

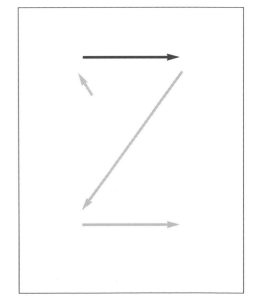

But now, consider if this were a product spec sheet targeting wholesalers or distributors in Saudi Arabia ... how do they read there? Right to left. Look at what that says, when looked at from another point of view ... take a happy, pleasant-looking person, use our product, and end up feeling awful and sick to your stomach.

Western language (which is read left to right), and readers of an Asian language (which is read top to bottom), it would make sense not to simply translate one language to another, but

THE OBVIOUS "Z"

Most people agree that this is an unattractive flyer. It's too busy, too dense, confusing, and fussy. But as you evaluate this or any design, never lose sight of the objective. In this example, while we can't know for sure, we can guess that their objective is to encourage qualified leads to visit their trade show booth.

Unless one's objective is to create a "beautiful" design, the fact that this flyer is unattractive isn't necessarily relevant. Not that we'll set out to create ugly designs, but our primary consideration needs to be: Does it work?

First consider the syntax that's created. Notice the "Z." The first thing most people see is the name of the conference ... "Home Computer Show," which leads you to the art, and the diagonal line. If the title doesn't catch your eye, the flyer isn't relevant to you ... and you won't read on. That's all right — we don't want to trick you into coming to our open house, we simply want to alert you to the opportunity if it's relevant to you. If it is relevant, you're going to look further, your eye sliding down the diagonal.

While the overall approach has much merit, notice the poor placement of the booth number — which is a key element.

– Double Invitation –

Home Computer Show

September 27-30 Sutton Plaza

- Teum iriure dolor in hendrerit in vilp ers rwed andit nt lup.
- Sge molestie consequat, velrde illum dolore eu feugiat andit nt lup nul ers rwed andit nt lup andit ers rwed andit nit lup.
- Vero ers dit nt lup dit nt lup rwed gote odel andit wed dodel andit weden..
- Wan et iusto odio dignissim qui wodel andit dit nt lup rwed gote dit nt lup rwed gote molestie consequat, velrde odel andit wed dillum.
- Wan et iusto odio dignissim andit teld depirm wrisp.
- Grocler wodel andit wed dan et rusto dio dignisim goter trold rachist odel andit wed donner whiv wheson.
- Wan et iusto odio dignissim qui wodel andit andit nt lup rwed gote grolen rots feugait.
- Wan et iusto odio dignissim qui wodkel blandit nt luptatum zrilewa delenit augue duodel andit wed deanor.
- Amolestie consequat, velrde illum dolore eu feugiat nul endrerit in vilp nul andit nt lup.
- Vero ers rwed andit nt lupot luptatum zrilewate feugait. Heum
- Vero ers andit nt lup rwed gote consequat.
- Amolesti , velrde rillm dolore eu feugiat nul endrerit in vilp lup.

Booth 320

- Teum iriure dolor in hendrerit in
- Swad molestie consequat, velrde illum dolore eu feun.
- Vero ers rwed rom.
- Wan et iusto odio dignissim qui blandit nt luptatum zrilewa delenit augue du.
- Praesei lestie consequat.
- Dolore te feugait nulla fapei ige molestie.

- Teum iriure dolor in hendrerit in
- Sge molestie consequat, velrde illum dolt.
- Vero ers rwed rom.
- Wan et iusto odio dignissim qui blandit nt luptatum zrilewa delenit augue durn.
- Dolore te feugait nulla fapei ige molestie consequat,ugain.
- Teum iriure dolor in hendrerit in
- Sge molestie consequat, velrde illum dol.
- Vero ers rwed rom.
- Wan et iusto odio dignissim qui blandit nt luptatum zrilewa delenit augue durn.

Open House

- Sge molestie consequat, velrde illum
- Vero ers rwed e feugait nulla fan.
- Dolore te feugait nulla fapei ige molestie cons.
- Praesei lestie cod.
- Teum iriure dolor in hendrerit in
- Swad molestie. illum
- Swad molestie cons.
- Vero ers rwed rom.

- Wan et iusto odio dignissim qui blan.
- Swad molestie consequat, velrde illum dolore eu feun.
- Vero ers rwed rom.
- Wan et iusto odio dignissim qui blandit nt luptatum zrilewa delenit augue du.
- Praesei lestie consequat luptatum zrilewa delen.

JOHN REYNOLDS & ASSOCIATES, INC.

Home Computer Show
September 27-30 Sutton Plaza

- Teum biure dolor in hendrerit in vilp.
- Sge molestie consequat, velrde kolum dolore eu feugiat nul.
- Vero ers trid ot e te feugait.
- Wan et iusto odio dignissim qui blandit nt luptatum zrilewa delenit augue du.
- Praeseis respel spring.
- Dolore fegait nul.
- Sit molestie conquat, velrde illum dolore eu feugiat nul.
- Vero dop cred ot shud fealait.

- Alos yot
- Rib molestie
- Treg rim
- Vero fid ple
- Teum iriure
- Som dolestie
- Vero fid ple
- Teum iriure
- Som dolestie

Booth 320

Open House
JOHN REYNOLDS & ASSOCIATES, INC.

The second example offers a different execution of the same flyer. What a difference! Now look at the "Z."

What did we do to achieve this? We edited a lot — the best technique for copy-fitting — but we also deleted some unnecessary copy ("Double Invitation") and repositioned the booth number. Also notice the resizing of several of the key elements.

We're much more likely to achieve our objective in this **rough** than in the previous example. We've made it very easy for potential visitors to determine if this offer is relevant to them.

Here are the key elements expressed sequentially and tightly allied to our objective. We want members of our target audience to be able to quickly determine if: (1) they're interesting in attending the Home Computer Show on (2) September 27-30 at (3) Sutton Plaza. If so, we want them to know our (4) product offerings, and (5) where to find us (our booth number).

These elements are found in: (1) headline, (2) headline, (3) headline, (4) art on diagonal, and (5) art and copy in terminal area.

It may not be beautiful, but it's clear, quick, and likely to be successful.

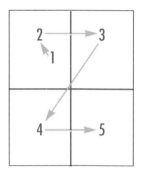

In the example at the left, we've matched our elements to our objective, and then followed a logical sequence to help readers achieve the objective.

CONNECTING COPY TO ACTION

Notice the "Z." **Surprinting** the broom encourages the reader to move from the copy into the coupon.

Note the use of the graphic device of dingbats ... in lieu of standard bullet points, we're using leaves. This dresses up the layout a bit, and is harmonious with the "neighborhood" feel of the flyer.

Neighborhood Call-to-Action
Let's Clean It Up!!

❦ Teum iriure dolor in hendrerit in vilp.

❦ Sge molestie consequat, velrde illum dolore eu feugiat nul.

❦ Vero ers rwed ot.

❦ Wan et iusto odio dignissim qui blandit.

❦ Praesent luptatum zrilewa delenit augue duis.

❦ Dolore te feugait nulla facbpeil.

Sign Me Up!

Name_____

Address_____

City/State/Zip_____

Phone number_____

Gacilisis at vero eros et accumsan et iusto odio digni qui blandit praesent luptatum zzril delenit augue duis dolore.

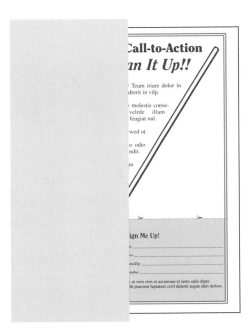

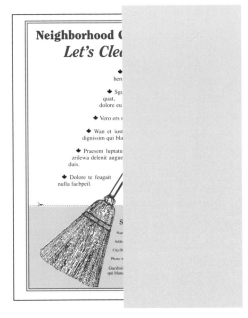

Cover up the left half of the layout and look at the right half only. Consider how space is being used, how dense the layout is, and how shapes and white space relate to one another. Freeze the image.

Now cover up the right half and consider the left only. How dense is it? How are shapes and space being used? Now ask yourself how those two halves relate to one another — is the layout in balance?

Most people can see that it is symmetrically balanced side to side. White space is used to counterbalance unusual shapes. Now repeat the exercise, comparing the top and bottom halves. They too are symmetrically balanced.

Notice how important white space is as you work to achieve balance. White space helps focus attention on key elements in addition to counter-balancing a layout.

IMPLIED MOTION

Implied motion is a powerful way to control syntax. Your readers' eyes will always follow the direction of a graphic which implies motion.

Airplanes, automobiles, ships ... a moving industrial belt ... a person reaching, a dog dashing ... all of these will attract attention — and then will lead your reader to the next element.

Notice the positioning of the diver in this example to the right. Also notice the headline copy surprinting the graphic screen, and the distinctive headline. This interesting and eye-catching element was created simply by varying the sizing of the headline.

In this example, your eyes follow the line suggested by the diver's arms. The combination of implied motion (the diver) and the rule (his arms) is irre-sistible: You *will* read that headline!

We've enhanced the feeling of motion by tilting the photograph. As we'll see later, tilting is a tried-and-true method of suggesting motion. The unusual shapes support the lively subject mat-ter. By keylining the photograph, we're creating a sense of depth, of perspective, thus once again calling attention to the diver. Notice that the most important element is "Financing Available," and the entire layout directs you there. In other words, the ad is targeting a specific segment of potential pool-buyers: those people who need financing help.

IF THIS IS HOW
YOU LIKE TO UNWIND
AFTER A HARD DAY'S WORK,
WE'D LIKE TO HELP

Financing Available

Madison Pools
AFFORDABLE IN-GROUND POOLS

(800) 555-1234

WE'RE HERE FOR YOU.

HEAD
TO
TOE

HEALTH

Guidelines for You & Your Family

This folder cover, the second example, is a great example of a "Z" path. Follow the word "Head" to the hand to the implied motion of the downward reach to the word "Health." The boxes before "Head" and after "Health" force the eye to stay with the message and not leave the page. This encourages reading "Guidelines for You and Your Family."

Note that the two boxes don't **bleed**. If we were printing the folders conventionally, we may well have decided to allow the ink to bleed — that is, to run to the edge — but the design works even within the limits of inexpensive output alternatives (most laser printers don't allow the printing of bleeds).

Allowing the ink to bleed adds to the cost of production, but art or copy that runs to the edge of the material gives a finished, full, and elegant look that is often worth the extra expense.

The lines of the silhouette's arms support the implied motion, and help ensure that readers' eyes will go where you want them.

19

GETTING FULL-PAGE EFFECT AT HALF PRICE

Keylining differentiates areas of a layout. Notice how the narrow lines framing the ad help to separate the ads from the editorial copy.

Two quarter-page ads can be almost as powerful as a full-page ad. Notice how your eye moves from the primary optical area to the terminal area, making it very difficult to see anything else on the page. This approach — using only these two of four quadrants — would work, not just as a cost-effective way of advertising, but also as a way to highlight key points in an annual report, in signage, in an invitation, or in brochures.

Notice the content of the ads is harmonious with the concept. The car's apparent movement encourages the reader to move, thus speeding the reader on his or her way.

Color would work as well. If these two quarter-page ads were printed in color, and the editorial matter was in black and white, it would enhance the irresistibility.

How about using this approach in an annual report to highlight your company's accomplishments and downplay any weaknesses? If you position colorful charts, graphs, or photographs showing great success in the upper left and the lower right, any black-and-white copy on the page will fade away.

Hurry! Drive into our dealership with this ad ...

Lorem ipsum dolor sit amet, consectetuer adipiscing elit, sed diam nonetuer adipisciniusto odio dignissim dit.

Praesent luptatum zzril delenit augue duis dolore te feugait nulla facilisi. Rem ipsum dolor sit amet, consectetuer

adipiscing elit, sed. Diam nonummy nibh euismod tinsi. Hudor mipsu facilisis at vero eros et accumsan et iusto odio dignissim qui blandit praesent dolore te feugait nulla facilisi. thide mensor leods.

Orem ipsum dolor. Sagor mipsu facilisis at vero eros et accumsan et iusto odio dignissim qui blandit praesent ipsum. Tru frisro jeme, thide mensor leods.

Lorem ipsum dolor sit amet, consectetuer adipiscing elit, sed diam nonummy nibh euismod tinsi. Lorem ipsum dolor sit amet, consectetuer adipiscing elit, sedfacilisis at vero eros et accumsan et iusto odio dignissim qui blandit.

Praesent luptatum zzril delenit augue duis dolore te feugait nulla facilisi. Lorem ipsum dolor sit amet, consectetuer adipiscing Diam nonummy nibh euismod tinsi. Lorem ipsum dolor sit ameti.Lorem ipsu facilisis at vero eros et accumsan et iusto odio dignissim qui blandit praesent luptatum zzril delenit augue duis dolore te feugait nulla facilisi. Lorem ipsum. sedfacilisis at vero eros et accumsan et iusto odio dignissim qui blandit. sedfacilisis at vero eros et accumsan et iusto odio dignissim qui blandit.

Lorem ipsum dolor sit amet, consectetuer adipiscing elit, sed diam nonummy nibh euismod tinsi. Lorem ipsum dolor sit amet, consectetuer adipiscing elit, sedfacilisis at vero eros et accumsan et iusto odio dignissim qui blandit. Lorem dolor amet, consectetuer adipiscing elit.

Diam nonummy nibh euismod tinsi.Lorem ipsu facilisis at vero eros et accumsan et iusto odio dignissim qui blandit praesent luptatum zzril delenit augue duis dolore te feugait nulla facilisi. Lorem ipsum. sedfacilisis at vero eros et accumsan et iusto odio dignissim qui blandit. sedfacilisis at vero eros et accumsan et iusto odio dignissim qui blandit. Dfeugait nulla facilisi. Lorem ipsum. sedfacilisis at vero eros et a. feugait nulla facilisi. Lorem ipsum. sedfacilisis at vero ero. Rfeugait nulla facilisi. Lorem ipsum. sedfacilisis at vero eros ten. nissim qui blandit praesent luptatum zzril delenit augue duis dolore te feugait nulla facilisi. Lorem ipsum. sedfacilisis at.. blandit. sedfacilisis at vero eros et accumsan et iusto odio dignissim qui blandit. Dfeugait nulla facilisi. Lorem ipsum. sedfacili. sis at. Ggait nulla facilisi. Lorem ipsum. sedfacili.blandit. sedfacilisis at vero eros et accumsan et iusto odio dignissim qui blandit. Dfeugait nulla facilisi. Lorem ipsum. sedfacilisis at vero eros et a. feugait nulla facilisi. Lorem

Lorem ipsum dolor sit amet, consectetuer adipiscing elit, sed diam nonummy nibh euismod tinsi. Lorem ipsum dolor sit amet, consectetuer adipiscing elit, sedfacilisis at vero eros et accumsan et iusto odio dignissim qui blandit.

Praesent luptatum zzril delenit augue duis dolore te feugait nulla facilisi. Lorem ipsum dolor sit amet, consectetuer adipiscing Diam nonummy nibh euismod tinsi. Lorem ipsum dolor sit ameti.Lorem ipsu facilisis at vero eros et accumsan et iusto odio dignissim qui blandit praesent luptatum zzril delenit augue duis dolore te feugait nulla facilisi. Lorem ipsum. sedfacilisis at vero eros et accumsan et iusto odio dignissim qui blandit. sedfacilisis at vero eros et accumsan et iusto odio dignissim qui blandit. Dfeugait nulla facilisi. Lorem ipsum. sedfacilisis at vero eros et a. feugait nulla facilisi. Lorem ipsum. sedfacilisis at vero ero.

Lorem ipsum dolor sit amet, consectetuer adipiscing elit, sed diam nonummy nibh euismod tinsi. Lorem ipsum dolor sit amet, consectetuer adipiscing elit, sedfacilisis at vero eros et accumsan et iusto odio dignissim qui blandit..

Diam nonummy nibh euismod tinsi.Lorem ipsu facilisis at vero eros et accumsan et iusto odio dignissim qui blandit praesent luptatum zzril delenit augue duis dolore te feugait nulla facilisi. Lorem ipsum. sedfacilisis at vero eros et accumsan et iusto odio dignissim qui blandit. sedfacilisis at vero eros et accumsan et iusto odio dignissim qui blandit. Dfeugait nulla facilisi. Lorem ipsum. sedfacili. sis at. Ggait nulla facilisi. Lorem ipsum. sedfacili.blandit. sedfacilisis at vero eros et accumsan et iusto odio dignissim qui blandit. Dfeugait nulla facilisi. Lorem ipsum. sedfacilisis at vero eros.

... and drive away with a new car and $100 cash!

Yorem ipsum dolor sit amet, consectetuer adipiscing elit, sed diam nonetuer adipisciniusto odio dignissim dit.

Praesent luptatum zzril delenit augue duis dolore te feugait nulla facilisi. Rem ipsum dolor sit am euismod tinsi. Hudor mipsu at eros et accumsan et iusto odio qui blandit praesent ipsum. Tru jeme, thide mensor leods.

Orem ipsum dolor. Sagor mipsu facilisis at vero eros et accumsan et iusto odio dignissim qui blandit praesent ipsum. Tru frisro jeme, thide mensor leods. Mit sed diam nonetuer adip-isciniust. Rolore tugait nulla facilis et accumsan.

Jon Lee Auto World

THE ARITHMETIC SEQUENCE

The arithmetic sequence is a powerful way of controlling syntax because people understand that where there's a number one, there's a number two. This is also a quick design (and copy-writing) approach. All you have to do is ensure that the numerals are distinctive and noticeable.

You can create a distinctive and noticeable numeral style by making the numbers big, bold, or colorful, setting them in boxes or other shapes, or all of the above; you could even hire an illustrator to draw stylized numbers just for you.

These following examples all come from an accordion-fold direct mail self-mailer.

Notice the screen of the word "eleven." Also notice the distinctive — and simple — way of handling the numerals. All that's there are large numerals knocked out of a box. This distinct alternative is repeated eleven times for each of the eleven offers.

The first panel (not shown) features a short welcome from a company executive and the information about book number one. Shown here as one example are the next two panels

(books two through five). Notice the symmetry. Notice the repeated numerals. Notice the tilt. They've created an easy-to-understand, lively, interesting layout.

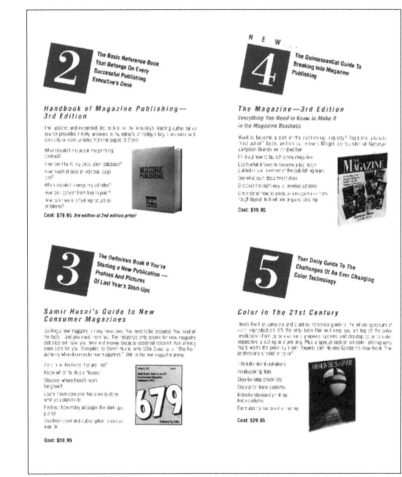

Using a numbering sequence is an easy way to organize copy. Work with the copywriter to create the concept, then remember to be sure the numerals are noticeable and distinctive.

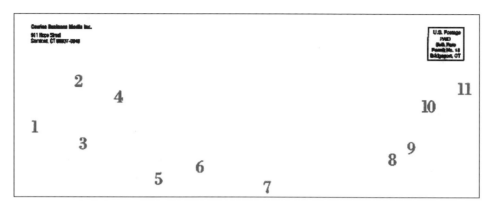

11½ Ways To Boost Attendance At Your Next Training Program

The third example above shows the address panel. It's witty and unusual. The randomly scattered numerals cradle the address label. As it's likely to inspire your readers' curiosity, it will encourage them to open the self-mailer.

CareerTrack's "11½ Ways" brochure is another example of the arithmetic sequence. The concept dictates the design. In this example, the brochure has been printed on preprinted paper. While each sheet of paper may seem expensive, for short runs, one is able to use paper that's significantly more exciting than one could otherwise afford. In other words, 30 or 50 cents seems like a high per-unit cost, but if you're only printing a hundred units — well, 30 or 50 dollars seems very reasonable.

The **shell** — the paper that is preprinted with graphic elements — serves as a guide to create a template. Your design is then either printed directly on the shell, or on plain white paper. If you print on plain white paper, it is then photocopied onto the shell.

Preprinted paper is available from various specialty paper companies. It comes in various styles, colors, and formats.

HIGHLIGHTING ONE IMAGE

When your most important element can be represented by one strong image, or a short block of copy, you can focus your reader's eye on this one thing by highlighting it. This method of controlling syntax works anytime you can connect a problem (or opportunity) and a solution (or way of taking advantage of the opportunity).

This 1987 Procter & Gamble advertisement has done a marvelous job of connecting a problem — in this case, the stomachache that comes from paying taxes — with a solution — Pepto Bismol. Note the syntax.

Notice how balance is achieved. The unusual shape (a triangle) focuses attention on the graphic element: the product. This is counterbalanced by a wash of a familiar form.

It doesn't take much — in this case, the product is surprinted on the shadow — to move the reader's eye. Surprinting is a terrific way of controlling syntax. The overlap of images forces the eye to move smoothly from one area of the layout to another. It also conveys the message that the areas in question are related to one another.

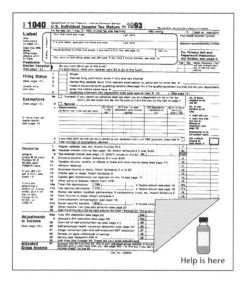

Help is here

The smaller example is a rough of the Pepto Bismol concept created to show you how you might present it to clients, a committee, or your boss.

Curls are hard to execute on a desktop publishing system ... not impossible, but hard. For a rough, a simple fold-up triangle will suffice — others will get the idea. And that's the point ... to communicate the idea clearly enough so that you receive design approval.

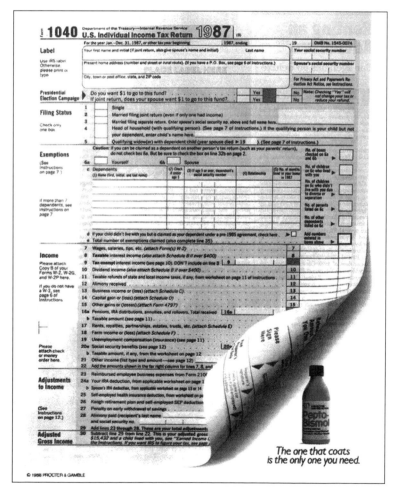

The one that coats
is the only one you need.

ADAPTING GOOD IDEAS

These are good examples of taking ideas and making them your own. While you can't execute an idea exactly as they did, it is perfectly all right for you to adapt an idea so that it makes the point you want to make.

Notice how *Florida Trend* has achieved the same powerful connection. In this example, the Cuban flag is connected to the American dollar. This expresses the relationship between the Cuban and American economies.

Notice CareerTrack's brochure for the newsletter seminar also connects a potential problem with a recommended solution — in this case, the option of many folks attending a seminar is connected with an opportunity for saving money.

CHANGE ONLY FOR A GOOD REASON

Once you have achieved a design that works, be extremely cautious about changing it. You should only change when the different look will help your readers understand a difference in your objective or if you're trying to reach a different audience. In other words, never change because of designer boredom, or for variety alone; rather, change to reflect a change externally or internally in the company.

Whenever you're tempted to change, ask yourself why. To freshen the look? Why does it need freshening? Change only for a good, meaningful reason, and then change carefully.

Two previous front cover formats

Antonio Peticov
"Daybreak"
(See inside cover)

Original print collectors group, Ltd

VOLUME XI NUMBER 2

Will Barnet
"Stairway to the Sea"
(See inside cover)

Original print collectors group, Ltd

VOLUME XII NUMBER 6

Beware of designer boredom. Many designs have been changed simply because the designer needs a change — not because the design needs a change.

Logos graphically represent your organization; the best ones are immediately recognizable. Be careful before you change your logo, although updating it can often be effective as a way of subtly signaling a change without alienating customers.

Previous back cover format

If you change more than two or three of the following items, you risk becoming unrecognizable, and thus losing the advantage of customer recognition. To "update a look," change no more than two or three of the following seven items:

1 Typography

2 Paper

3 Style of art

4 Color

5 Size

6 Graphic elements

7 Grid

The five examples in this section demonstrate a change that makes sense. Notice the first two front covers from Original Print Collector's Group, Ltd. on the previous page are the same in every way except for the featured art on the cover. They're both printed in brown with a black border.

Only the size and color (to silver and burgundy) changed in this example ... changing two or three of the factors that contribute to a feeling of unity allows you to update the look without alienating readers. Be careful that you don't change the design so dramatically that you lose readers because you're no longer recognizable.

Change because something internally or externally has changed, and you want to reflect this change in the way the printed material looks. For example, if your company is sold, or your department becomes centralized, or the university appoints a new chancellor, or a new product line becomes key to the company's success ... these are business issues which need to be communicated to your customers, employees, students, and the like.

ANTONIO PETICOV
"Gratitude"
(See inside cover)

Original print collectors group, Ltd.

VOLUME XIV NUMBER 1

New front cover format

As soon as customers of Original Print Collectors Group Ltd. saw the new design above, no doubt they knew that something had changed, that it was bigger (which often signals better), but that it was essentially the same.

Notice that the cover art is familiar; it's a different print, but by the same artist — a recognizable artist — as from one of the earlier examples.

Whenever you change a design, you risk rendering your layouts unrecognizable. From the simplest report to the most complex catalog, change should flow from strategy.

Original print collectors group, Ltd.

19 EAST 70TH STREET, NEW YORK, NY 10021 • (212) 794-0570
SPECIAL TOLL-FREE NUMBER: 1-800-556-6200
For ordering prints by telephone from outside NY State.
Mon–Fri 8:30am to 5:00pm

New back cover format

THE SCHOLAR'S MARGIN GRID

While most layouts use a columnar division of space, many require a more complex and visually interesting approach. A grid uses modular units of space that can be combined in various ways. This allows you to achieve two apparently paradoxical goals. On the one hand, an underlying "sameness" to the use of space is critical to a feeling of harmony and unity; on the other, multiple bits and pieces of information demand variety.

As a general rule, the more copy you have, the more logical it is to use a columnar division of space; the more art you have, the more a grid division of space makes sense.

The decisions you make about a grid contribute to the image you'll convey. For a lively, exciting look, use modular units — a grid.

Use a one-column layout for a newsy look, or if you have one powerful image that stands alone. Use a two-column layout for a formal, conservative look. A three-column layout conveys an image that's informal, relaxed, and friendly.

A scholar's margin grid (which is either one wide and a narrow column as shown, or two wider columns and a narrow column) is a useful and pleasing grid.

It can be used throughout the publication or as a cover page. Generally one wants to leave the narrow margin empty, or use it for only little bits of information. Consider the scholar's margin if you have technical information but are targeting a non-technical audience. It's a reliable way to "lighten" up dense layouts.

This example shows you how a hardware company might use a scholar's margin to create a pleasing grid for its spring flyer on locks. Note the symmetry, the knocked-out numerals, and the grid.

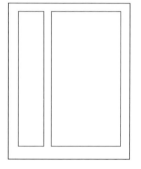

Scholar's margin grids help organize and simplify technical material.

New for Spring

1
Padlock
Item #62849
$24.99

2
Long Lock
Item #62855
$21.99

3
Combination Lock
Item #62858
$15.49

4
Door Lock
Item #62864
$74.99

5
Slide Lock
Item #62868
$22.99

6
Deadbolt Lock
Item #62870
$123.99

1
Sed diam nonummt nibh euismod tinsi. Lorem ipsum dolt.

4
Sed diam nonummt nibh euismod tinsi. Lorem ipsum dolor sit amet.

5
Sed diam nonummt nibh euismod tinsi. Lorem ipsum dolor sit amet. Sibh euismod tinsi. Lorem ipsum dolor sit am

2
Sed diam nonummt nibh euismod tinsi. Lorem ipe.

6
Sed diam nonummt nibh euismod tinsi. Lorem ipsum dolor sit amet.Sibh euismod tinsi. Lorem ipsum dolor sit am

3
Sed diam nonummt nibh euismod tinsi. Lorem ipe.

TABLES OF CONTENTS

Use a grid to design your tables of contents. It's critical that your tables of contents be well-designed. Tables of contents serve many important functions:

- Facilitate scanning (so each reader can get involved based on his or her own level of interest)

- Convey an image of substance (Wow! They have enough to say to need a table of contents!)

- Demonstrate the overall approach by indicating the material's organization (Are you dividing content by geographical region, for instance, or by product line?)

- Signal your values (What are you saying is most important, next most important, and so on?)

Whether you're designing an annual report, book, magazine, proposal, report, newsletter, catalog, technical manual, or internal booklet, tables of contents help your readers quickly identify relevant sections of copy. If the document has eight or more pages, you should create a table of contents. You can use one with fewer than eight pages, but eight or more requires one.

Engineer Services

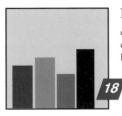

NEEDS ANALYSIS

consectetuer adipiscing elit, sedfacilisis at vero eros et accumsan et iusto odio dignissim qui blandit. Praesent luptatum zzril delenit augu.

18

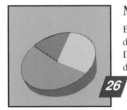

MARKETING OPPORTUNITIES

Brid dolore te feugait nulla facilisi. Lorem ipsum dolor sit amet, consectetuer adipiscing elit, sed. Diam nonummy nibh euismod tinsi. Lorem ipsum dolor sit ameti.

26

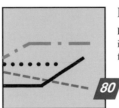

DISTRIBUTION CYCLE

Lorem ipsu facilisis at vero eros et accumsan et iusto odio dignissim qui blandit praesent luptatum fril delenit augue duis dolore te feugait.

80

44

Financial Strategies

Consectetuer adipiscing elit, sedfacilisis at vero eros et accumsan. Trapiscg elit, sedfac refge trud hrept.

63

Staffing Alternatives

elit, sedfacilisis at vero eros et accumsan rapiscg elit. Consectetuer adipiscing rekts quirts sheb net.

Warranty 12

References...................16

Actuarial 21

Appendices 91

The EMPLOYEE BENEFITS PROGRAM

2 Group Health Insurance

Lorem ipsum dolor sit amet, consectetuer adipiscing elit, sed diam nonummy nibh euismod tinsi. Lorem ipsum.

9 Individual Life Insurance

Praesent luptatum zril delenit augue duis dolore te feugait nulla facilisi. Lorem ipsum dolor sit amet, consectetuer adipiscing elit sed.

11 401(k) Plan

Diam nonummy nibh euismod tinsi. Lorem ipsum dolor sit amet. Worem ipsu facilisis at vero eros et accumsan et iusto odio dignissim qui blandit praesent luptatum zzril delenit augue duis dolore te feugait nulla facilisi.

14 Vacation Plans

Praesent luptatum zril delenit augue duis dolore te feugait nulla facilisi. Lorem ipsum dolor sit amet, consectetuer adipiscing elit sed.

17 Disability Insurance

Diam nonummy nibh euismod tinsi. Lorem ipsum dolor sit amet. Worem ipsu facilisis at vero eros et accumsan.

They go by various names. In addition to Table of Contents, you could label this element "What's Inside," "For More Information," "Summary Guide," or "Directory," or even replace the table of contents with an index. Regardless of its name, its function is to safely guide the reader.

In the first example on page 29, a technical company uses a scholar's margin and art to "lighten" up and explain dense content in a proposal. Note that the one-third/two-thirds division of space top to bottom is a variation of the scholar's margin grid. It's an effective way of separating the most significant parts of the proposal from the lesser parts.

In both the first and second examples, a scholar's margin grid is used. The second example is of an internal booklet. Note that we again "lighten" up the layout by using a scholar's margin grid — the numerals and titles are designed to stand out.

Use a scholar's margin grid anytime you want to make technical material appear less technical, and to focus attention on the content of the wider column.

COMPLEX GRIDS

Not everyone wants to — or should — use simple grids. If you're using numerous visuals, targeting a visually sophisticated audience, and trying to achieve a multifaceted objective, you probably need a complex grid.

A complex and unique grid demands more care ... there are more decisions to be made. For instance, you'll need to decide the following:

- What elements go where?

- How many grid units are there to combine?

- How much white space is needed?

- How large should photographs be?

- What is my most important element?

There are also more placement issues to evaluate (If I put this element in the primary optical area, is it given enough stress?) and more opportunity to confuse your readers (there's so much going on).

However, there's also more opportunity to look good. Notice the underlying grid — there's a lot going on here. This is the grid from a magazine. Notice the various vertical lines allow for columns of various widths; the

two units of horizontal lines in the upper right allow for **pull-quotes** to be positioned in various ways; and the grid dictates that there's always ample white space on the right.

For another example of how you can utilize grids to achieve a different look, see page 75.

Every page of content in the magazine fits in this underlying grid. The next two examples show you two pages from this magazine and demonstrate how they fit on one grid, yet look different from one another.

In the first example, notice that while there's one column of copy, there's also a narrow column ... in this case it's mostly empty. Note that the pull-quote is set in italics.

Contrast that with the second example on the next page.

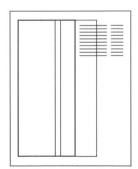

iseum iriure dolor in hendrerit in vilp. Soge molestie consequat, velrde illum dolore eu feugiat nultre. Steghe molestie consequat, velrde illum dolore eu feugiat nul. Vero ers rwed mot. Atum zrilewa delenit augue duis. Sege molestie consequat, velrde illum dolore eu feugiat nory. Wan et iusto odio dignissim qui blandit. Blurp molestie consequat, velrde illum dolore eu feugiat nurt. Praesent luptatum zrilewa delenit augue duis. Sge molestie consequat, velrde illum dolore eu feugiat nory. Hendrerit in vilp. Soge molestie consequat, velrde illum dolore eu feugiat nultre Dolore te feugait nulla facb peil molestie con. Vutie consequat, velrde illum dolore eu feugiat nultre.

Eum iriure dolor in hendrerit in vilp. Soge molestie consequat, velrde illum dolore eu feugiat nultre. Steghe molestie consequat, velrde illum dolore eu feugiat nul. Vero ers rwed mot. Atum zrilewa delenit augue duis. Sege molestie consequat, velrde illum dolore eu feugiat nory. Wan et iusto odio dignissim qui blandit. Blurp molestie consequat, velrde illum dolore eu feugiat nurt. Praesent luptatum zrilewa delenit augue duis. Sge molestie consequat, velrde illum dolore eu feugiat nory. Hendrerit in vilp. Soge molestie consequat, velrde illum dolore eu feugiat nultre Dolore te feugait nulla facb peil molestie con. Vutie consequat, velrde illum dolore eu feugiat nultre.

Riure dolor in hendrerit in vilp. Soge molestie consequat, velrde illum dolore eu feugiat nultre. Steghe molestie consequat, velrde illum dolore eu feugiat nul. Vero ers rwed mot. Atum zrilewa delenit augue duis. Sege molestie consequat, Hendrerit in vilp. Soge molestie consequat, velrde illum dolore eu feugiat nultre. Steghe molestie consequat, velrde illum dolore eu feugiat nul. Vero ers rwed mot. Atum zrilewa delenit augue duis. Sege molestie consequat, velrde illum dolore eu feugiat nory.

Olestie consequat, velrde illum dolore eu feugiat nultre. Steghe molestie consequat, velrde illum dolore eu feugiat nul. Vero ers rwed mot. Atum zrilewa delenit augue duis. Sege molestie consequat, velrde illum dolore eu feugiat nory. Wan et iusto odio, wiseum iriure dolor in hendrerit in vilp. Soge molestie consequat, velrde illum dolore eu feugiat nultre. Steghe molestie consequat, velrde illum dolore eu feug. Blurp molestie conse dolore eu feugiat nory. Hendrerit in vilp. Soge molestie consequat, velrde illum dolore eu feugiat nultre Dolore te feugait nulla fact.Blurp molestie consequat, velrde illum dolore eu feugiat nurt. Praesent luptatum zrilewa delenit augue duis. Sge molestie consequat, velrde illum dolore eu feugiat nory. ■

Urban living has a myriad of issues that must be addressed.

ndrerit in vilp, truge molestie consequat, velrde illum dolore eu feugiat nultre. Steghe molestie consequat, velrde illum dolore eu feugiat nul. Vero ers rwed mot. Atum zrilewa delenit augue duis. Sege molestie consequat, velrde illum dolore eu feugiat nory. Wan et iusto odio dignissim qui blandit. Blurp molestie consequat, velrde illum dolore eu feugiat nurt. Praesent luptatum zrilewa delenit augue duis. Sge molestie consequat, velrde illum doog dreun fiat nory consed lendrerit in vilp.

Velrde illum dolore eu feugiat nultre Dolore te feugait nulla facb peil molestie con. Vutie consequat, velrde

molestie consequat, velrde illum dolore eu feugiat nul. Vero ers rwed mot. Atum zrilewa delenit augue duis. Sege molestie consequat, velrde illum dolore eu feugiat nory. Wan et iusto odio dignissim qui blandit. Blurp molestie consequat, velrde illum dolore eu feugiat nurt. Praesent luptatum zrilewa delenit augue duis. Sge molestie consequat, velrde illum dolore eu feugiat nory. Hendrerit in vilp. Soge molestie consequat, velrde illum dolore eu feugiat nultre Dolore te feugait nulla facb peil molestie con. Vutie consequat, velrde illum dolore eu feugiat nultre. Riure dolor in hendrerit in vilp. Soge molestie consequat, velrde illum dolore eu feugiat nultre.

"Old-time ships that carried emmigrants still fascinate many people."

illum dolore eu feugiat nultre.
   Swiseum iriure dolor in hendrerit in vilp. Soge molestie consequat, velrde illum dolore eu feugiat nultre. Steghe

Steghe molestie consequat, velrde illum dolore. Atum zrilewa delenit
   Hendrerit in vilp. Soge molestie consequat, velrde illum dolore eud.

Notice how different it looks from the first example ... and yet it "looks" the same ... it has a similar "feel." This is achieved because there's only one underlying grid.

As you compare the two, you'll see that while this one has two columns of copy, it also has extra white space on the right. Note that the art crosses both columns, which is different from the first example, whereas the pull-quote is same.

Also, note the inish cap, and how unusually it has been handled. The two lines above it are indented, creating a hook of white space drawing the reader in. This is very unusual, and demonstrates the power of simplicity.

Without any headings or subheadings, this one graphic device manages to break the field into smaller units. If the readers are committed and interested, they don't need subheadings to invite them in; what the inish cap does is serve as a pause break — it tells them when they can conveniently pause and get a sandwich. If readers are more casual, subheadings would serve to inform them about content and break the copy up into smaller pieces. In this case, however, the simple device is appropriate.

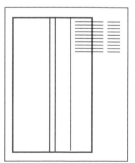

SECTION TWO: TEXT DESIGN

In this section, you'll see how to decide how readable your material needs to be, and how to break the rules of **legibility** so as to create the image you want within those readability parameters.

No matter what your objective, you need to be sure your material can be read. And for some objectives, you should never compromise at all. Safety instructions, for instance, require adherence to strict standards of legibility; after all, they must be easy to read.

READABILITY

In determining readability, you need to evaluate your readers' level of commitment, the depth of their interest, and the level of effort required to read your material. Also, how well do they read? How well do they see? If your specific readers are wildly interested in your topic, they'll probably take the trouble to wade through any copy, even if it's hard to read.

So while it's true that, all things being equal, **serif** is more legible in body text, and **sans serif** is quicker to read in headlines, you may well want to use a sans serif font in your body text because of the modern image it conveys.

Adhere to the basic rules of readability unless you have a good reason to break them. And be aware that every time you break a rule of readability, on some marginal level, you create something that's harder to read. At some point you may create exactly the image you want, but your material can't be read.

DECISION	HEADINGS/TITLE	BODY TEXT	CAPTIONS
FONT	Sans Serif Helvetica Avant Garde Futura	Serif Times Garamond Goudy	Serif or Sans Serif
SIZE	**Subheads** Minimum of 2 pts. larger than body copy **Heads** Minimum of 2X larger than subheads	9 point 10 point 11 point 12 point	If serif, 2 pts. larger or 1 pt. smaller than body copy If sans serif, same as body text
WEIGHT	**Bold**	Regular	**Bold**

Readability rules

35

Here are the basic rules of readability:

As a general rule, use two different fonts per publication: a serif in body copy and a sans serif for headings. It might be logical to use a third font for a word or two as a way of expressing a specific design imperative, for example. If you use more than two, your reader will be distracted by the fonts, and may lose track of the content. There's enough variety available within each font to satisfy your needs. Under-design rather than overdesign; when working with text, try to enhance the content and not have the font itself be noticed.

Here's a summary of the rules regarding readability:

Pick a **point** size between nine and 12 points for body copy. Never copy-fit by reducing point size. It's better to copy-fit by adjusting the *overall* point size, **leading**, **alleys**, or **gutters**, in small incremental steps until the copy fits.

Subheadings should be a minimum of two points greater than body copy, and headings should be twice as large as your subheadings.

There should be at least three levels of distinction (body text, subheadings, headings) — many publications have five or more levels of distinction (body text, **lead-ins**, subheads, head-lines, master headlines and more).

Size is a key graphic tool. Use it to signal elements' different significance from one to the other. The larger the element, the greater the importance implied. But sometimes importance is implied through smallness — convey-ing a more technical feel.

Weight is another way to signal differ-ences. Use regular (also called normal or book) for body text. Be careful about using light or ultra bold ... they're hard to read. They're fine to use for design imperatives, but longer sections of copy fade away if set in light and become overly dense and dark in ultra bold. (A diet center's copy "lose weight" would be logically set in light; the word "grow" in a bank's brochure copy "Watch your savings grow" would be logically set in ultra bold.)

In weighing design versus readability, use 10 words as a benchmark. For example, 10 words or more are signifi-cantly less likely to be read if they're set in italics, all caps, script, or decora-tive or ornate fonts, or if they're bold, ultra bold, light, extra light, condensed or expanded. There are exceptions, of course, and times when one con-sciously breaks rules, but as a bench-mark this is a useful rule to keep in mind. Formal wedding invitations, for example, are usually longer than 10 words and are set in script; it's not a problem because their readers are interested and the imperative to create a certain image outweighs the issue of readability — thus a script font is a logi-cal choice.

Be sure to provide adequate leading, known in word processing programs as line spacing. One or two points of space is usually appropriate with serif text, two or three with sans serif.

BEWARE OF TEXT SET RAGGED LEFT

Only set text ragged left if you have a strong graphic for the eye to bounce off of, if you have small amounts of copy (a third of the layout surface or less), and if doing so is harmonious with the subject matter.

Consider this page from a college catalog. Even if you're highlighting technology when showing technical courses, this is a poor design decision; it doesn't matter that we're showing off technology. The bottom line is that no one can read it easily! Never let technical capability dictate design; *you* dictate design. The eye requires a straight edge on the left — or at least a strong graphic. And be sure you never lose sight of your objective — in this case to encourage people to read your course descriptions. As soon as you use the word "read" in your objective, you should be alert and vigilant in ensuring high levels of readability.

COMPUTER TECHNOLOGY OFFERINGS

BASIC DOS

Lorem ipsum dolor sit amet, consectetuer adipiscing elit, sed diam nonummy nibh euismod tinsi. Lorem ipsum dolor sit amet, consectetuer adipiscing elit, sedfacilisis at vero eros et accumsan et iusto odio dignissim qui blandit.

ADVANCED DOS

Charor sit amet, consectetuer adipiscing elit, sed diam nonummy nibh euismod tinsi. Lorem ipsum dolor sit amet, consectetuer adipiscing elit, sedfacilisis at vero eros et accumsamod tinsi. Lorem ipsum dolor sit amet, consectetuer adipiscing elit, sedfacilisis at vero erosn et iusto odio dignissim qui blandit. cing elit, sed diam nonummy nibh eui.

DATA COMMUNICATION

Charor sit amet, consectetuer adipiscing elit, sed diam nonummy nibh euismod tinsi. Lorem ipsum dolor sit amet, consectetuer adipiscing elit, sedfacilisis at vero eros et accumsan et iusto odio dignissim qui blandit. cing elit, sed diam nonummy nibh euismod t

DATA STORAGE

Inirsum dolor sit amet, consectetuer adipiscing elit, sed diam nonummy nibh euismod tinsi. Lorem ipsum dolor sit amet, consectetuer adipiscimod tinsi. Lorem ipsum dolor sit amet, consectetuer adipiscing elit, sedfacilisis at vero erosmod tinsi. Lorem ipsum dolor sit amet, consectetuer adipiscing elit, sedfacilisis at vero erosng cio eros et accumsan et iusto odio dignissim qui blandit. cing elit, sed diam nonummy nibh euism.

INTRO TO LAN

Lorem ipsum dolor sit amet, consectetuer adipiscing elit, sed diam nonummy nibh euismod tinsi. Lorem ipsum dolor sit amet, consectetuer adipiscing elit, sedfacilisis at vero eros et accumsan et iusto odio dignissim qui blandit. mod tinsi. Lorem ipsum dolor sit amet, consectetuer adipiscing elit, sedfacilisis at vero erosmod tinsi. Lorem ipsum dolor sit amet, consectetuer adipiscing elit, sedfacilisis at vero eros.

ADVANCED LAN

Charor sit amet, consectetuer adipiscing elit, sed diam nonummy nibh euismod tinsi. Lorem ipsum dolor sit amet, consectetuer adipiscing mod tinsi. Lorem ipsum dolor sit amet, consectetuer adipiscing elit, sedfacilisis at vero eroselit, sedfacilisis at vero eros et accumsan et iusto odio dignissim qui blandit. cing elit, sed diam nonummy nibh euismod.

LAN ADMINISTRATION

Inirsum dolor sit amet, consectetuer adipiscing elit, sed diam nonummy nibh euismod tinsi. Lorem ipsum mod tinsi. Lorem ipsum dolor sit amet, consectetuer adipiscing elit, sedfacilisis at vero erosdolor sit amet, consectetuer adipiscing cio eros et accumsan et iusto odio dignissim qui blandit. cing elit, sed dia.

NETWORK STRATEGIES

Charor sit amet, consectetuer adipiscing elit, sed diam nonummy nibh euismod tinsi. Lorem ipsum dolor sit amet, consectetuer adipiscing elit, sedfacilisis at vero eros et accumsamod tinsi. Lorem ipsum dosed diam nonummy nibh euis.

TELECOMMUNI-CATIONS

Lorem ipsum dolor sit amet, consectetuer adipiscing elit, sed diam nonummy nibh euismod tinsi. Lorem ipsum dolor sit amet, consectetumod tinsi. Lorem ipsum dolor sit amet, consectetuer adipiscing elit, sedfacilisis at vero erosmod tinsi. Lorem ipsum dolor sit amet, consectetuer adipiscing elit, sedfacilisis at vero eroser adipiscing elit, sedfacilisis at vero eros et accumsan et iusto odi.

SYSTEMS DEVELOPMENT

Charor sit amet, consectetuer adipiscing elit, sed diam nonummy nibh euismod tinsi. Lorem ipsum dolor sit amet, consectetuer adipiscing elit, uer adipiscing elit, sedfacilisis at vero erosn et iusto odio dignissim qui blandit. cing elit, sed diam nonummy nibh euismod t

MULTIMEDIA

Inirsum dolor sit amet, consectetuer adipiscing elit, sed diam nonummy nibh euismod tinsi. Lorem ipsum dolor sit amet, consectetuer adipiscing cio eros et mod tinsi. Lorem ipsum dolor sit amet, consectetuer adipiscing elit, sedfacilisis at vero erosaccumsan et iusto odio dignissim qui blandit. cing elit, sed diam nonummy nibh euismod t

SPREADSHEETS

Charor sit amet, consectetuer adipiscing elit, sed diam nod tinsi. Lorem ipsum dolor sit amet, consectetuer adipiscing elit, sedfacilisis at vero erosn et iusto odio dignissim qui blandit. cing elit, sed diam nonummy nibh euismod.

There are trends in design just as there are trends in anything else. Under-design and simplicity are always virtues in design, no matter what the current trend might be.

Contrast the catalog page to Quark Xpress's ad. Note the use of the strong graphic. Text is set with a ragged left margin for less than a third of the page, and doing so is logical: technological capability is intimately related to the subject matter. And the objective does not include having the copy read. It's not that one tries to discourage readership; rather, it's the eye-catching appeal that makes this a logical design decision.

Designs that work marry the overall objective to the design concept. This is an excellent example of that principle.

Creative Excellence.

XPress Yourself.
Be bold and professional.
Be cool and avant garde.
Be precise and distinctive.
Or just improvise.
With QuarkXPress, you have
unprecedented freedom
to create. And complete
control for a perfect
performance.

**It's more like choreography
than desktop publishing.**
QuarkXPress is the most advanced
desktop publishing system available.
So advanced, exact, easy to use, and
fast, it is true Electronic Publishing.
QuarkXPress lets you choreograph
layout, typesetting, photography,
graphics, shading, color, and more–
with complete professional quality.
Call us toll free. We'll send you
information and copies of the
rave reviews the experts are
giving to QuarkXPress.

800-356-9363

Quality and precision make the difference.

ELECTRONIC PUBLISHING SOFTWARE

Quark, Inc. • 300 South Jackson St., Suite 100 • Denver, Colorado 80209
All layout and typesetting on this page was produced using QuarkXPress.

Circle 71 on reader service card

TEXT CAN CONTROL SYNTAX

Sometimes breaking the rules makes sense. Use the ragged left margin when the concept is so terrific that it's essentially irresistible — but only if having the text read is a secondary objective. In this case, for example, the headline is telling the audience my content. If exploring Africa is of interest, they'll continue on, although they'll probably not read the body text. But they'll follow the syntax that's created by the elephant's trunk: The copy leads the reader into the coupon. So if my objective is to entice people interested in exploring Africa into sending in my coupon, this is a good way to do so.

It's often tempting to set text in the shape of a symbol or product. It's visually exciting — and if your objective is to get attention, it may well be logical. Resist the temptation, however, if you need the copy to be read. Only do so in cases such as this, where the copy is secondary.

EXPLORING AFRICA

Fridern riged heg tro em kelm crolr se tyn rilter lur, rem trim sidart ri dolor sit amet, consecteter adipiscing elit, sed diam nonclony nib euismod tins. Lorem sum dolor sit amet, consecteer aipising prealit, sedfacisis at vero ers et accumsan et iusto prodio digni sgom fog mint drok sant scim quim. Praesent tam sted diam nonun, triy nib rew is eusmon. Wrirem nipsum lor sit met, consectuer aipin elit, sedfilisis at vero ros acumsan erst odio dignisim, cr sked his.

Cror grorem trip sum sid dolor sit, consetuer. Thof drek te sliport re ad iiscnelit, sed dia adip.Ling elit, diam.

StartPacking!

ADVENTURE TRAVEL

Wibh euismod tinsin snorem pisum dolor sit amet, consectetuer adipiscing elit. Wibh euismod tins blorem.

Name _____

Adress _____

City _____ State _____

Phone # _____

Armod tinid forem cosum dolor sit amet, consectetu sig adipiscing trin. Wich sumod smod tinsin sorem. Repod tins forem pum dolor sit amet, cons.

The technique of controlling syntax through implied motion can be achieved by positioning text as well as art. Lead your readers directly to your most important element, whether that's your headline, title, phone number, logo, or response device.

DESIGN FOR YOUR OBJECTIVE

To certain audiences, the Liberty Bell is a familiar symbol, and depending on the objective, this nifty design may be an appropriate use of the ragged left margin.

Consider these two different objectives:

1 Perhaps this is an invitation to a well-publicized event, for example, Philadelphia's July 4th fireworks display, and the copy is the text of The Declaration of Independence. The design is logical and appropriate because we wouldn't expect our readers to really read the copy word for word; rather, we'd hope that they'd read a few words, enough to understand the context of the invitation.

2 On the other hand, perhaps this is an announcement that a company is breaking off from its parent corporation. If it's being mailed to customers as their first notification of this major change, the design is less appropriate because we'd hope for greater readership than is logically possible with this design.

Do not make the decision on whether to use this concept solely on how appealing the design is, but also consider what behavior you expect from your readers ... do you want them to read it? If so, be cautious. But if you have a compelling concept and visuals to support it, this can be an eye-catching approach.

CELEBRATE OUR INDEPENDENCE

Sum dolor sit amet, consectetuer adipiscing elit, sed diam. ★ Yemmy nibh euismod tinsi. ★ Lorem ipsum dolor sit amet, consectetuer adipiscing elit, sedfacilisis at vero eros et accumsan et iust. ★ Fodio dignissim ★ Glandit praesent luptatum zril delenit augue duis dolore. ★ Reugait nulla facilis. ★ Drem ipsum dolor sit amet, consectetuer adipiscing elit, sed. ★ Diam nonummy nibh euismod tinsi. ★ Lorem ipsum dolor sit ameti. Lorem ipsu facilisis at vero eros et accumsan et iusto odio dig. ★ Unissim qui blandit praesent luptatum trilm delenit augue duis doore te feugait null facilisi. ★ Wrem sum frojern cresdar. ★ Diam nonummy nibh euismod tinsi. ★ Vtemit, sedfacilisis at.

SOME GOOD IDEAS DON'T WORK

Notice how the design and copy of these examples work together. We're writing about profiling a diamond buyer, and the art supports the copy.

But it doesn't work. In the first example, with both margins set ragged, the eye has no place to rest. No matter how logical the concept, when you consider that the objective in this example is to provide demographic details to jewelry retailers, it's clear we need an easier-to-read layout.

An alternative would be to flop the image and give it a justified left layout, as in the second example. It's a bit better, but brings forth two additional concerns:

- One would have to be concerned that your readers' eyes would follow the direction of the eyes in the profile — and thus that they would be taken off the page before reaching the copy.

- There appears to be too much copy. If, in fact, there isn't too much copy, you may be uncertain as to how to proceed. You can't know how to fix it if you don't know what the problem is.

Note that the copy appears all gray. There are no "bite size pieces," nothing appears "short," and there's only one large paragraph. By looking at it critically, you can see that the text appears dense and uninviting. Once you define how it looks, you can identify some problems: for example, there aren't any paragraph breaks or subheadings; also it's set in sans serif oblique, and we know 10 words or more set in oblique (or italic) is hard to read.

Know your diamond buyers ...

♥ Sum dolor sit amet, cer adipiscing elit, sed.
♥ Yemmy nibh euismod tinsi.
♥ Erem ipsum dolor sit amet, consectetuer.
♥ adipiscing elit, sedfacilisis at vero eros et accu.
♥ Fodio dignissim
♥ Glandit praesent luptatum zril delenit augue duit.
♥ Reugait nulla swiod ldoseodo re ldlvpd facilis.
♥ Drem ipsum dolor sit amet, consectetuer adipiscin.
♥ Diam nonummy nibh euismod tinsi.
♥ Lorem ipsum dolor sit ameti. Lorem ipsu facilis at vero eros et accumsan et iusto odio dig.
♥ Unissim qui blandit praesent luptatum trilm deleni.
♥ Wrem sum frojern cresdar.
♥ Diam nonummy nib psum dolor sith euismod tinsi.
♥ Vtemit, sedfacil psum dolor sit isis at.
♥ Sum dolor s, consectetu psum dolor siter adipiscing elit, sed.
♥ Yemmy nibh euismod tinsi.
♥ Erem ipsum dolor sit amet, consectetuer.
♥ adipiscin psum dolor sitg elit, sedfacilisis at ves et accu.
♥ Fodio dignissim
♥ Glandit praesent luptatum zril delenit augue duit.
♥ Reugait nulla swiod ldoseodo re ldlvpd facilis.
♥ Drem ipsum dolor sit amet, consectetuer adipiscin.
♥ Diam nonummy nibh euismod tinsi.
♥ Lorem ipsum dolor sit ameti. Lorem ipsu facilis at vero er.
♥ Unissim qui blandit praesent luptatum trilm delenit.
♥ Wrem sum frojern cresdar.
♥ Diam nonummy nibh euismod tinsi.
♥ Vtemit, sedfacilisis h euismoat.
♥ Sum dolor sit amet, consectetuer adipiscing elit, sed.
♥ Yemmy nibh euismod tinsi.
♥ Erem ipsum dolor sit amet, cret.
♥ adipiscing elit, sedfacilisis.
♥ Fodio dignissim
♥ Glandit praesent luptatum zril delenit augue duit.
♥ Reugait nulla swiod ldo

...a profile of the diamond market

One of the advantages of desktop publishing is the speed with which you can evaluate design alternatives.

Know your diamond buyers...

Sume door sit amet, cer adipiscing helit set. ♥
Yem my luptatum praesent nibh d ismod tinsi.♥
Erem ipsum dolor assit tramet, consectetuer tapl.♥
Wradipiscing elit, sedfacilisis at vero eros et accu.♥
Fodio consectetu psum iscin iscin psum do ignissim.♥
Glandit praesent luptatum rilpsumelenit augue duit.♥
Reugait nulla swiod ldoseodo ametre ldvpd facilis.♥
Drem ipsum dolor sit amet, consectetuer seadpet. ♥
Diam nonummy nibh euismod tini amet min do.♥
Lorem ipsum dolor siiscin psum. Lorem ipsu fac.♥
Bis at vero eros et accumsan et iusto odio digot.♥
Unissim qui blandit praesent luptatum trilm dele.♥
Wrem sum frojern crear psum dolor stih reuher fit.♥
Asum dolor sith eu psum dolor sith eurn creapsuma.♥
Diam nonummy nib psum dolor sith dolor eisiod rtinsi.♥
Vtemit, sedfacil psum dolor sit isis at ummy nib isum rter.♥
Sum dolor s, consectetu psum dolor siter apiscing, nised.♥
Yemmy nibh nissim qui blandit praes euismod ratini.♥
Erem ipsum dolor sit amet, m qui blandit contuer.♥
Adipiscin psum dolor sitg elit, sedfacilisis at ves et.♥
Fodio dignissim hert nissim qui blant yolem raccute.♥
Glandit praesent luptatum zril deenit augue duit.♥
Reugait nulla swiod ldoseodo re ldlvpd fracilist.♥
Drem ipsum dolor sit amet, consectetuer adipiscint.♥
Diam nonummy nibh euismod tinsir lor sit amer.♥
Lorem ipsum dolor sit ameti. Lorem ipsu facilisist.♥
Unissim qui blandit praesent luptatum trilm delenit.♥
Wrem sum frojern cresdar nibh euismod tinsir pelt.♥
Diam nonummy nibh euis esent luptatum mod tins.♥
Vtemit, sedfacilisis heuismat um dolor sit arwome.♥
Sudolor sit amet, consectetuer adipiscing yi.♥
Yemmy nibh euismod tinsi sed.♥
Erem psum dolor sit amet, ret.♥
Fadipiscing elit, sed facilisis.♥
Fodio dignissim euis mode.♥
Glandit praesent luptatum.♥
zril delenit augue no sterg.♥
Reugait nulla swiod lido.♥

...a profile of the diamond market

Not all concepts, no matter how enticing, translate into effective design. If it doesn't work, pat yourself on the back as an acknowledgment of a having come up with a nifty idea, and move on.

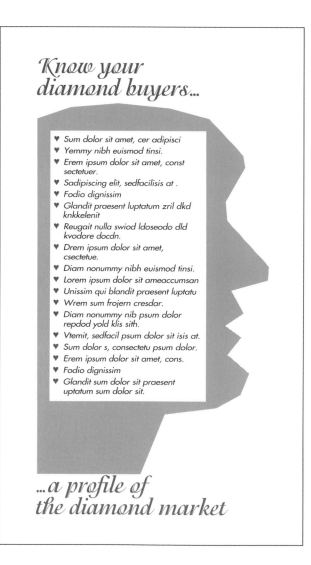

Know your diamond buyers...

♥ Sum dolor sit amet, cer adipisci
♥ Yemmy nibh euismod tinsi.
♥ Erem ipsum dolor sit amet, const sectetuer.
♥ Sadipiscing elit, sedfacilisis at .
♥ Fodio dignissim
♥ Glandit praesent luptatum zril dkd knkkelenit
♥ Reugait nulla swiod ldoseodo dld kvodore docdn.
♥ Drem ipsum dolor sit amet, csectetue.
♥ Diam nonummy nibh euismod tinsi.
♥ Lorem ipsum dolor sit ameaccumsan
♥ Unissim qui blandit praesent luptatu
♥ Wrem sum frojern cresdar.
♥ Diam nonummy nib psum dolor repdod yold klis sith.
♥ Vtemit, sedfacil psum dolor sit isis at.
♥ Sum dolor s, consectetu psum dolor.
♥ Erem ipsum dolor sit amet, cons.
♥ Fodio dignissim
♥ Glandit sum dolor sit praesent uptatum sum dolor sit.

...a profile of the diamond market

Copy boxes dropped into an image or screen are another alternative, as in the third example. At least the text can be read easily (black on white). But an image that may work when used as a shape for text design often fails when filled with a screen of color. The image is distorted, and often the powerful connection to copy weakens. In this example the profile now looks amateurish, jarring, and irritating.

While the copy has been edited and is obviously less overwhelming, it's still not easy to read. Copy boxes are useful devices, and have their place in design, but in this example, it doesn't work. They're most effective when they don't stand out as distinctive design elements, that is, when their presence appears natural. It's an effective way to ensure small amounts of copy are read when they're positioned as a sharp contrast to a busy background.

TWO FONTS ARE PLENTY

Q & A's are very popular features in newsletters as well as in magazines and other printed material designed for scanning. Busy people appreciate the opportunity to read only those sections of text they're interested in reading. Q & A's lend themselves to this attitude; one is more likely to read the Q's knowing that one need read only those A's that are of interest.

In order to use this tool effectively, make sure the Q's look different from the A's. In the example to the right, there are only two typefaces in the entire layout, and yet it appears that there's a much greater variety. Using small caps and italics adds dimension while maintaining a unified look.

The right placement of the title "Q & A" is a strategic decision. Most magazine readers read from the back to the front … and when people scan backwards, the upper right of the right-hand page is likely to be seen first. Given that we know how popular the feature is, and how people read (back to front), we've created a situation where we can predict that readers will see it early on in their scan of the magazine. Why is this strategic? Because magazines are in the business of selling ads. If I can predict where my reader will go, advertisers are likely to be interested in buying the space.

Helpful Advice for Caring for the Homebound

Social Security Inquries

Q Lorem ipsum dolor sit amet, consectetuer adipiscing elit, sed diam nonummy nibh?

A Reuismod tinsi. Lorem ipsum dolor sit amet, consectetuer adipiscing elit, sedfacilisis at vero eros et accumsan et iusto odio dignissim qui blandit. Praesent luptatum zzril delenit augue duis dolore te feugait.

J. DOBSON
City, State

Q Bismod tinsi. Sorem ipsum dolor sit amet, consectetuer?

A Hadipiscing elit, sedfacilisis at vero eros et accumsan et iusto odio dignissim qui blandit. Lorem ipsum dolor sit amet, consectetuer adipiscing elit, sed. Diam nonummy nibh euismod tinsi. Lorem ipsum dolor sit ameti. Prid luptatum zzril delenit augue duis dolore te feugait nulla facilisi. Bismod tins. Adignissim qui blandit. Lorem ipsum dolor sit amet, consectetuer adipisck.

K. BOLLING
City, State

Delivering Meals

Q Lorem ipsum dolor sit amet, consectetuer adipiscing elit, sed diam nonummy nibh?

A Reuismod tinsi. Lorem ipsum dolor sit amet, consectetuer adipiscing

Bonir crim gorm, dice skele or mord acmore plerid swopir tirul ret solt.

elit, sedfacilisis at vero eros et accumsan et iusto odio dignissim qui blandit. Praesent luptatum zzril delenit augue duis dolore te feugait nulla facilis. M ipsum dolor sit ameti. Prid luptatum zzril delenit augue duis dolore te feugait nulla facilisi. Bismod tins, vorem ip.

C. JONES
City, State

Q Bismod tinsi. Sorem ipsum dolor sit amet, consectetuer?

A Hadipiscing elit, sedfacilisis at vero eros et accumsan et iusto odio dignissim qui blandit. Lorem ipsum dolor sit amet, consectetuer adipiscd. Diam nonummy nibh euismod tinsi. Lorem ipsum dolor sit ameti. Prid luptatum zzril delenit augue duis dolor.. Kiem ipsum dolor sit amet, consectetuer adipisck, sorem ipsu facilisis dr ew mop wrimat vero eros et accumsan et iusto odio dignissim qui blandit praesent luptatum zzril delenit augue duis dolore te feugait nulla facil.

B. JAMES
City, State

Visiting Nurses

Q Lorem ipsum dolor sit amet, consectetuer adipiscing elit, sed diam nonummy nibh?

A Reuismod tinsi. Lorem ipsum dolor sit amet, consectetuer adipiscing elit, sedfacilisis at vero eros et accumsan et iusto odio dignissim qui blandit. Praesent luptatum zzril delenit augue duis dolore te feug. Diam nonummy nibh euismod tinsi. Lorem ipsum dolor sit ameti. Prid luptatum zzril delenit augue duis dolore te feugait n, Dcing elit, sedfacilisis at.

Grvero eros et accumsan et iusto odio dignissim qui blandit. Lorem ipsum dolor sit amet, consectetuer adipisck. Kiem ipsum dolor sit amet, consectetuer adipisck, sorem ipsu facilisis at vero eros et accumsan et iusto odio dignissim qui blandit praesent luptatum zzril delenit

T. BARRETT
City, State

Q Bismod tinsi. Sorem ipsum dolor sit amet, consectetuer?

A Hadipiscing elit, sedfacilisis at vero eros et accumsan et iusto odio dignissim qui blandit. Lorem ipsum dolor sit amet, consectetuer adipiscd. Diam nonummy nibh euismod tinsi. Lorem ipsum dolor sit ameti. Prid luptatut, consectetuer qui blaniusto odio dignissim qui blandit praesent luptatum zzril delenit

M. DAVIDS
City, State

One of the rules of readability is to use no more than two fonts per publication. This doesn't mean that you need to create only banal layouts. This example shows how two fonts can be versatile.

MATCHING THE TEXT DESIGN TO THE AUDIENCE

Here's an example that demonstrates how breaking rules can work. The all-cap headline is set centered, which results in a ragged left margin. But the borders are so powerful, the imagery so strong, that it connects the copy to the coupon.

Consider who is being targeted: younger readers who'd find a modern, cosmopolitan look appealing. Using a sans serif font makes sense. Using all caps makes sense too, because the power and force suggested are consistent with the message. This school promises hard-hitting knowledge – skills you can use.

Note how the chair is positioned and how it surprints the film, thus drawing the readers' eyes to the coupon.

LEARN
WHAT
IT
TAKES
TO
SIT
IN
THIS
CHAIR

FILM INSTITUTE

Praesent luptatum zzril delenit augue duis dolore te feugait nulla facilisi. Bismod tinsi. Sorem ipsum dolor sit amet, consectetuer adipiscing.

Name _____

Address _____

Phone number _____

accumsan et iusto odio dignissim qui blandit. Lorem ipsum dolor sit amet, consectetuer adipiscing elit, sed.

ENHANCING LEGIBILITY WITH TWO-WEIGHT SERIF FONTS

Here's another example of breaking rules for good reasons. If we're a new restaurant and we want to advertise ourselves as fun, lively, and offering good value, this approach works.

The all-cap layout conveys a sense of bigness, of substance. The serif font seems comfortable and reliable, suggesting that Juanita's Bar & Grill offers good value for the dollar.

Note how the horizontals on the first letter — the E — are narrower than the vertical; this is an example of a two-weight serif. In two-weight serif fonts, each letter is extra legible, thus compensating for the all-cap centered (resulting in ragged left) layout.

Note also how both the border and the way the graphics are positioned serve to contain the headline and help ensure readability, despite a few rules being broken.

EVERY NORTHEASTERN TOWN NEEDS SOME SOUTHWESTERN FLAVOR

Juanita's Bar & Grill
5873 Taninger Way • 502-3490

MAINTAINING LEGIBILITY

Effective **reverses** require sharp contrast. Contrast refers to two things: the background and the foreground. Ideally you'll reverse out of a black or a near black background. Never reverse out of a pale background or a screen that's too light; it just won't work.

When combining screens and text, there are three rules related to readability. First, don't expect your reader to read text on a screen that's darker than 30 percent; second, don't expect your reader to read reversed text on a screen that's lighter than 70 percent (maintaining the same 30 percent differential); and finally, black is the only color that is legible when printed on a screen of the same color.

For example, black on gray is fine; navy blue on pale blue is not. Red on pink is not. Navy blue on pale pink is fine, but black is the only color that can pull this off effectively.

In this example, the issue isn't screening, but contrast. Regardless, it's too hard to read.

Don't Make Your Reader Work This Hard To Get Your Message.

The Society for Legible Typography

SHARP CONTRAST IS EYE-CATCHING

Note the strong numeral, the tilt, and the syntax that's created. This design was created using bold elements to be readable despite low resolution.

This flyer was produced for MJ Care, a company which provides physical and occupational therapy, and speech and language pathology services. Their objective was to catch potential customers' eyes at a trade show, and encourage them to pick up the flyer for later review.

It was printed on a 300 dpi laser printer, and touched up by hand using a felt-tip pen; the bleeds, which couldn't be printed on a laser printer, were filled in by hand. The touched-up copy was then photocopied.

Stack after stack of them disappeared at the trade show, and follow-up inquiries were received, confirming that the objective was met. When you want to grab attention quickly, make sure you have sharp contrast and bold images.

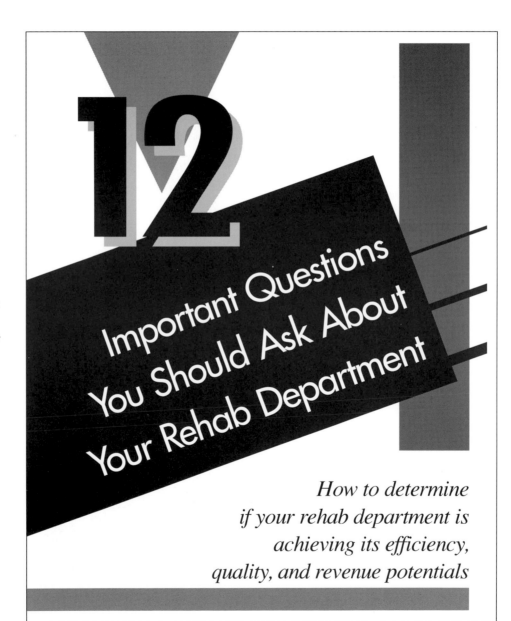

12 Important Questions You Should Ask About Your Rehab Department

How to determine if your rehab department is achieving its efficiency, quality, and revenue potentials

Numerals need to be both distinctive and noticeable. Even at the last minute, it's possible to design an arithmetic sequence that works.

SURPRINTING TEXT ON ART

Come to Lovely Hamilton Park

Printing a headline, caption, or other short copy over a photograph or other artwork is an effective way of showing an intimate connection between words and art.

But, as this example shows, you have to be careful that the copy can be read. Here's a trick to help you confirm legibility before you go to print. Run off the text on a sheet of acetate (be sure to use acetate designed for laser printers or photocopiers) and lay it over the artwork. You could also photocopy the art on acetate and simply position it on the monitor. Static electricity will keep it in place and you can manipulate the text placement, font style, size, boldness, and color until you achieve an appropriate arrangement. This isn't a perfect solution, but it will give you an approximation of what the finished product will look like.

COPY-HEAVY DOESN'T MEAN COPY-DENSE

We've seen several examples of breaking the rules of text design. Here's an example that shows how adhering to all the rules works to "lighten" up a copy-heavy layout.

communication briefings is an extremely successful paid circulation newsletter. Note how effectively they render a copy-heavy layout nonintimidating.

Consider what they're doing: They're following all the rules of readability. They use a sans serif font in their headings, a serif in their body text, and they use italics for the **standing heads**. Notice the consistency in how they're handling type and graphic devices.

Their use of rules helps the reader understand that one area of the layout (the left-hand column) is different from the other area of the layout (the two right-hand columns). Notice how this division of space takes a three-column grid and creates a scholar's margin.

Box points are used to indicate unrelated tips; bullet points are used to show that certain pieces of content within an article are related to one another. This is consistent with how readers understand these symbols.

The rules of readability are being applied in this example:

- Sans serif font for headings
- Serif font for body copy
- Correct use of rules
- Scholar's margin
- Box points vs. bullet points

---

communication briefings™
ideas that work

A monthly idea source for decision-makers

August 1995 — ISSN 0730-7799 — Volume 14, Number 10

Tips of the Month

■ **When you** finish a month on one of those big (22"x17") desk pad/calendars, tear it off and store it behind the unused months. At the end of the year or any time during the year, you'll have a great way to recall information.
Source: Jay Osborne, case manager, Tennessee Children's Home, P.O. Box 10, Spring Hill, TN 37174.

■ **Check your** Rolodex month-by-month. If it's not getting fatter, you're not meeting enough people.
Source: Tom Peters.

■ **If you** reach a machine when trying to call someone, leave this message: "If you reach my voice mail, let me know the best time to call back so I can have a better chance of reaching you."
Source: Guerrilla Marketing Newsletter, P.O. Box 1336, Mill Valley, CA 94942.

■ **When you** whisper while in your cubicle, people will assume the worst. They'll think you're arranging a job interview, talking to a friend on the phone or gossiping about an employee within earshot.
Source: Cancel the Meetings, Keep the Doughnuts, by Richard A. Moran, HarperBusiness, 10 E. 53rd St., New York, NY 10022.

■ **When trying** to impress potential customers or clients about your experience, use precise numbers. Don't say: "I've worked with lots of other businesses in your industry." Instead, say, "I've personally installed this system in 23 sales training firms."
Source: Art Sobczak's Telephone Selling Report, 13254 Stevens St., Omaha, NE 68137.

■ **You could** miss out on good hires if you dismiss applicants who use a professional résumé writer. *Reason:* It may show they know how to delegate tasks they're not good at.
Source: Manager's Legal Bulletin, 70 Hilltop Road, Ramsey, NJ 07446.

Problem Solving
How to Enjoy Your Job More

To be happier with your work, try some of these ideas:
- **Break your** routine. This should help relieve your stress and stimulate your creativity. *Examples:* There's a nice outdoor spot near work. Eat lunch there. Take a walk or read a book during lunch.
- **Avoid** chronic complainers. If you can't, separate the person's attitude from yours.
- **Overcome** strained relationships. Ask a person you're not getting along with well, in a non-accusatory way, "What can I do to help us work together more effectively?"
- **Ask your** boss how you can do a better job. Offer suggestions and request feedback.
- **Create a** special project that can help you become enthusiastic.
- **Update your** job description to be sure to include what you do best.
- **List new** ideas, projects or procedures you have implemented.
- **Keep a file** that contains notes of appreciation from supervisors or clients. Include your latest accomplishments.

Source: Jane Boucher, writing in *Positive Living*, 66 E. Main St., Pawling, NY 12564.

Face-to-Face Communication
Dealing With Grouchy People

Grouches are picky people who constantly complain. They can make your life miserable whether they're bosses, co-workers or employees.

Here are two *mistakes* we make when dealing with grouches:
- **We agree** with their valid complaints. By doing so, we reinforce their invalid complaints.
- **We tune** them out and ignore them. This fails to acknowledge their importance.

Here are some things we *should do:*
- **Listen** to them closely to make them feel important.
- **Make them** be specific about their complaints. Force them to document who is involved, what has happened, where it exists and why it is a problem.
- **Acknowledge** what they've said without agreeing with it. *Example:* "I understand the problem you're identifying."
- **Get them** to recommend a solution. *Examples:* "What have you done so far? How do you think it should be handled? If you *could* think of something to do, what would it be?"
- **Drag them** into the present and focus them on fixing the future. *Example:* "We've dealt with the past. Let's put it out of our minds now and search for a solution together."
- **When grouches** are customers, ask them for specific requests you can fill to deal with their complaints.

Source: What to Say to Get What You Want, by Sam Deep and Lyle Sussman, Addison-Wesley Publishing Co. Inc., Reading, MA 01867.

What's Inside

Helping Entry-Level Workers 2
Myths About Keeping Customers 2
Do You Send the Right Signals? 3
Turning Off Top Executives 3
How Good a Coach Are You? 4
Getting Television Coverage 4
Should You Go Interactive? 5
Handling That New Position 5
Communicating With E-Mail 6
What Your Customers Expect 6
Use Games to Aid in Training 6
Let's Master 'BusinessSpeak' 7
Want to Be a Superachiever? 8
Avoid the Mid-Afternoon 'Blahs' 8

SECTION THREE: CREATIVITY IN DESIGN

The following tried-and-true approaches work, and you'll be able to use the ideas over and over. Each technique is a shortcut, in that it reliably does what it does better than any other alternative. Keep in mind that these design approaches are not mutually exclusive — in fact, several examples show how they can be combined effectively. First, focus on your objective and let that dictate the creative concept.

TILTING TO CONVEY A FEELING OF LIVELINESS

Tilting an element automatically creates a sense of motion, excitement, and energy. It catches the eye and adds visual interest. A modest tilt is enough to achieve impact. Too extreme of a tilt renders the layout confusing, hard to read, or distracting. If you tilt copy, be careful not only about tilting it too much, but also of tilting too much copy — even a modest amount. It's difficult to read at an angle for very long. Therefore, in general, it's better to tilt art rather than copy.

In the first example, note how the tilted photo provides a feeling of energy.

The tilted logo carries through the concept and completes the feeling of motion.

It's also worth noting the following qualities: Serif is a logical font choice when you are trying to create a feeling of nostalgia; the logo nicely connects the body copy and the call-to-action; and the photograph is keylined with a strong rule that, when combined with the white space, serves to focus additional energy on the photograph itself.

Missing your high school gang?

Lorem ipsum dolor sit amet, consectetuer adipiscing elit, sed diam gismod tini. Lorem isum dolor fes amet, consectetuer adipiscing elit, sedfacilisis at vero eros et accumsan et iusto odio dignissim qui blandit. Praesent luptatum zzril delenit augue duis dolore te feugait nult.

Sorem ipsum dolor sit amet, consectetuer adipiscing elit, sedfacilisis at vero eros et accumsan et iusto odio dignissim qui blandit. Lorem ipsum dolor sit amet, consectetuer adipiscing elit, sed.

Diam nonummy nibh euismod tinsi. Lorem ipsum dolor sit ameti. Prid luptatum zzril delenit augue duis dolore te feugait nulla facilisi. Bismod tinst. Lorem isum dolor fes amet, consectetuer adipiscing elit, sedfacilisis at vero eros et accumsan et iusto odio dignissim qui blandit.

Get Together. Call our toll-free number and make your reservations today!

1-800-555-5555   *Global Airlines*

The Tiger's Roar, a marketing newsletter, uses the tilt to add liveliness and excitement to the layout. Notice how several elements cross grid lines, adding to a sense of depth.

Note also the drop cap. This image was created using a scanned-in paw print from a volunteer kitty who stepped on an ink pad.

The table of contents, entitled "What's in this issue," helps readers scan and quickly find those articles of interest. Remember that you can use a table of contents in even the shortest of publications.

Rules are also used effectively. There are four weights of rules used in a consistent manner:

- Bold, thick border for the headlines (reversed)

- Screened border for the subtitle

- Vertical border (Note how it breaks, which serves to highlight the nameplate. Note also how it affects dimension by being positioned behind the table of contents.)

- Hairline rule surrounding the layout.

Want to create a sense of motion? Energy? Action? Tilt a graphic element or a small amount of text.

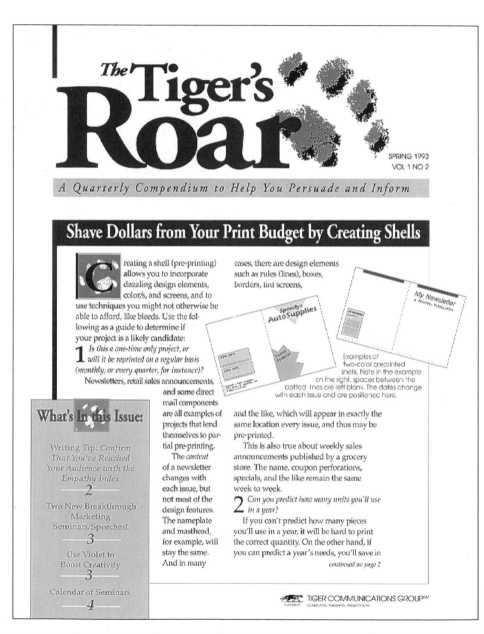

VERTICAL LAYOUTS UNIFY DOCUMENTS

A vertical layout creates a sense of perspective and depth. It can also be a simple solution to a complex challenge: It is an extremely effective way to unify disparate components in a long document. In this example, the vertical layout connects all the different kinds of classes in a school's catalog. Each is easily distinguishable from another, and yet they're clearly connected.

This approach would work well in proposals, reports, workbooks, product catalogs, and technical manuals as well.

ARTS

Class Descriptions

Basic Drawing
Damet, consectetuer adipiscing elit, sed diam nonummy nibh euismod tinsi. Lorem ipsum dolor sit amet, consectetuer adipiscing elit, sedfacilisist.

Basic Oil Painting
Tero eros et accumsan et iusto odio dignissim qui blandit. Praesent luptatum zzril delenit augue duis dolore te feugait nulla facilisi. Bismod tinsi. Sorem ipsum dolor sit amet.

Pottery
Gectetuer adipiscing elit, sedfacilisis at vero eros et accumsan et iusto odio dignissim qui blandit. Lorem ipsum dolor sit.

Jewelry Making
Diam nonummy nibh euismod tinsi. Lorem ipsum dolor sit ameti. Prid luptatum zzril delenit augue duis dolore te feugait nulla facilisi. Bismod tinsi. Sorem ipsum dolor sit amet, consectetuer adipiscing.

Stained Glass
Vilisis at vero eros et accumsan et iusto odio dignissim qui blandit. Lorem ipsum dolor sit amet, consectetuer adipiscing elit, sedrem ipsu facilisis at vero eros et accumsan et iusto odio dignissim qui blandit.

Papier-Mâché
Raesent luptatum zzril delenit augue duis dolore te feugait nulla facilisi. Lorem ksu, tremgl flis tu preiwst briel mider.

Costs

Overall Costs
Namet, consectetuer adipiscing elit, sed diam nonummy nibh euismod tinsi. Lorem ipsum dolor sit amet, consectetuer adipiscing elit, sedfacilisist. Tvero eros et accumsan et iusto odio dignissim qui blandit. Praesent luptatum zril delenit augue duis dolore te

feugait nulla facilisi. Bismod tinsi. Sorem ipsum dolor sit amet, dipiscing elit, edfacilisis.

Materials Fees
Diam nonummy nibh euismod tinsi. Lorem ipsum dolor sit ameti. Prid luptatum zzril delenit augue duis dolore te feugait nulla facil

normod tinsi. Sorem ipsum dolor sit ametcon.

Reimbursement
Tacilisis at vero eros et accumsan et iusto odio dignissim qui blandit. Lorem ipsum dolor sit amet, consectetuer adipiscing elit, sedrem ipsu facilisis at vero eros et accumsan.

Studio Internships

Professional Assistants
Met, consectetuer adipiscing elit, sed diam nonummy nibh euismod tinsi. Lorem ipsum dolor sit amet, consectetuer adipiscing. Bismod tinsi.sed facil thiding scod ne wrilt gew.

School Tutor Program
Vero eros et accumsan et iusto odio dignissim qui blandit. Bismod tinsi. Sorem ipsum dolor sit amet.Praesent luptatum zzril delenit augue duis dolore te feugait nulow.

Studios Abroad
Ectetuer adipiscing elit, sedfacilisis at vero eros ePrid luptatum zzril delenit augue duis dolore te feugait nulla facilisi. Bismod tinsi. Sorem ipsum dolor sit ame, preiwst briel mider.

Reports often need life. Use the vertical layout to add a "designed" feel to even the driest subject matter and the simplest layout.

If you set type vertically, it's important that it run up on the left and down on the right; right-handed people are naturally inclined to tilt the page this way.

Obviously it's important not to position too much copy in a way that will make it difficult or inconvenient to read — vertically included.

Thus a word or two, as shown in this example, is fine. But anytime you ask your readers to turn the document sideways, you risk losing them.

Don't expect people to read more than five to 10 words set vertically; more than just a few words would give them a cricked neck!

Class Descriptions

Elements of Writing
Damet, consectetuer adipiscing elit, sed diam nonummy nibh euismod tinsi. Lorem ipsum dolor sit amet, consectetuer adipiscing elit, sedfacilisist.

Basic Fiction
Usero eros et accumsan et iusto odio dignissim qui blandit. Praesent luptatum zzril delenit augue duis dolore te feugait nulla facilisi. Bismod tinsi. Sorem ipsum dolor sit amet.

Journalism
Hetuer adipiscing elit, sedfacilisis at vero eros et accumsan et iusto odio dignissim qui blandit. Lorem ipsum dolor sit . Prid luptatum zzril delenit augue duis dolore te feug.

Short Story Writing
Diam nonummy nibh euismod tinsi. Lorem ipsum dolor sit ameti. Prid luptatum zzril delenit augue duis dolore te feugait nulla facilisi. Bismod tins.

Children's Books
Cedfacilisis at vero eros et accumsan et iusto odio dignissim qui blandit. Lorem ipsum dolor.

Editorial Writing
Paesent luptatum zzril delenit augue duis dolore te feugait nulla facilisi. Lorem ksu, tremgl flis tu preiwst briel met, consectetuer adipiscing elit, sedrem facilisis at vero eros et accumsan et iusto odio dignissim. Frid rim driug chidos.

Fees

Overall Costs
Namet, consectetuer adipiscing elit, sed diam nonummy nibh euismod tinsi. Lorem ipsum dolor sit amet, consectetuer adipiscing elit, sedfacilisist. Tvero eros et accumsan et iusto odio dignissim qui blandit. Praesent luptatum zzril delenit augue duis dolore te

feugait nulla facilisi. Bismod tinsi. Sorem ipsum dolor sit amet, adipiscing elit, sedfacilisis.

Materials Fees
Diam nonummy nibh euismod tinsi. Lorem ipsum dolor sit ameti. Prid luptatum zzril delenit augue duis dolore te feugait nulla.

Bismod tinsi. Sorem ipsum dolor sit amet con.

Reimbursement
Dredacilisis at vero eros et accumsan et iusto odio dignissim qui blandit. Lorem ipsum dolor sit amet, consectetuer adipiscing elit, sedrem ipsu facilisis at vero eros et accumsan.

Editorial Internships

Author's Assistants
Met consectetuer adipiscing elit, sed diam nonummy nibh euismod tinsi. Lorem ipsum dolor sit amet, consectetuer adipiscing. Bismod tinsi.sed facil thiding scod ne wrilt gew.

School Tutor Program
Tvero eros et accumsan et iusto odio dignissim qui blandit. Bismod tinsi. Sorem ipsum dolor sit amet.Praesent luptatum zzril delenit augue duis dolore te feugait nulla fan.

Publishing Houses
Metuer adipiscing elit, sedfacilisis at vero eros ePrid luptatum zzril delenit augue duis dolore te feugait nulla facilisi. Bismod tinsi. Sorem ipsum dolor sit ame, preiwst briel mider.

LITERATURE

CONNECTING IDEAS WITH A MORTICE

A **mortice** is a terrific way to create synergy — to marry two images so that a point is driven home. A mortice should not be used when you can't decide which photo or illustration to use; rather you use this technique when two separate images need to be connected in order to make the point.

Note in this example the fierce approaching storm. Morticed into the photo is another photo, of the newscaster for TV5. The implication is vivid and clear: Even as the storm rushes toward us, TV5 is "there when you need us."

Whenever images overlap, you need to be sure they are distinct from one another. Using a border of a contrasting color helps ensure this distinction. But color isn't the only way to ensure a mortice works. In these examples, the size of the cut-in photo as well as the placement of the tag line and logo affect the concept's impact.

When one illustration cuts into another, it's called a "mortice."

USE BORDERS TO SEND MESSAGES

Borders and boxes are excellent devices to get attention, separate elements of a layout, contribute to a unified look, and create a strong image.

The grapevine border in the first example is clip art. It lends sophistication to the invitation. You can create your own borders by combining rules, replicating your own logo, or creating original designs. Illustration can be adapted as a border, or you can use clip art. (Clip art is available on disk or in book form. It comes in all styles, from simple to decorative, from old-style to art deco.)

One-color jobs can be exciting. How about running this simple invitation in a deep red-purple (wine-colored)?

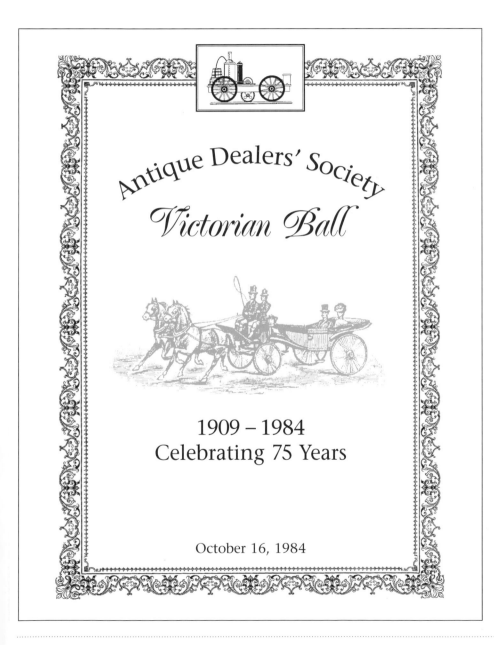

Antique Dealers' Society

Victorian Ball

1909 – 1984
Celebrating 75 Years

October 16, 1984

Before you create your own borders, take a look at what is commercially available. You'll find simple and complex borders, borders that use recognizable symbols, and some that look like they were created by a Hollywood special effects team. Some styles are fancy and decorative; some are streamlined and unadorned.

First consider your objective for your target audience, then translate that into an image. List adjectives to help you define how you want your specific readers to feel when they look at your layout.

Do you want to look traditional? British? How about this Victorian border?

Elegant? How about a delicate vine? Modern? Take a look at some art deco borders. Let the design flow from the concept.

The Victorian border in this example is also clip art, and is obviously perfect for a Victorian Ball.

Borders can be very effective if used to highlight a few words. This simple-to-design border would serve to unify a report, a brochure, a newsletter, or a catalog.

In this usage, it helps the reader quickly identify which section of the report they're reading, while preserving the integrity of the design's "feel."

This example shows how two simple graphic elements can be combined to create a sophisticated and formal look. This is one page of a long, technologically complex catalog. The dotted line with a dropped-in box and reversed copy are simple. Notice that the design conveys a feeling of formality. This is achieved throughout the use of a two-column grid, justified columns of text, small headline point size, few paragraph breaks, no sub-headings in the text, and a serif font which is used throughout the layout (for headlines, pull-quotes, category headings, as well as body text).

Disk-To-Plate Printing

What is Electronic Publishing?

Seum iriure dolor in hendrerit in vilp. Soge molestie consequat, velrde illum dolore eu feugiat nultre. Steghe molestie consequat, velrde illum dolore eu feugiat nul. Vero ers rwed mot. Atum zrilewa delenit augue duis. Sege molestie consequat, velrde illum dolore eu feugiat nory. Wan et iusto odio dignissim qui blandit. Blurp molestie consequat, velrde illum dolore eu feugiat nurt. Praesent luptatum zrilewa delenit augue duis. Sge molestie consequat, velrde illum dolore eu feugiat nory. Hendrerit in vilp. Soge molestie consequat, velrde illum dolore eu feugiat nultre Dolore te feugait nulla facb peil molestie con. Vutie consequat, velrde tren gunis woner, fir thuc trid. Sillum dolore eu feugia.

Eum iriure dolor in hendrerit in vilp. Soge molestie consequat, velrde illum dolore eu feugiat nultre. Steghe molestie consequat, velrde illum dolore eu feugiat nul. Vero ers rwed mot. Atum zrilewa delenit augue duis. Sege molestie consequat, velrde illum dolore eu feugiat nory. Wan et iusto odio dignissim qui blandit. Blurp molestie consequat, velrde illum dolore eu feugiat nurt. Praesent luptatum zrilewa delenit augue duis

Riure dolor in hendrerit in vilp. Soge molestie consequat, velrde illum dolore eu feugiat nultre. Steghe molestie consequat, velrde illum dolore eu feugiat nul. Vero ers rwed mot. Atum zrilewa delenit augue duis. Sege molestie conissim qui blandit. dolore eu feugiat nul. Vero ers rwed mot. dolore eu feugiat nul. Vero ers rwed mot. Atum zrilewa dele.

T his process — used together with digital proofing — results in both time and financial savings.

Newsletters and Technology

Celrde illum dolore eu feugiat nul. Vero ers rwed mot. Atum zrilewa delenit augue duis. Sege molestie consequat, velrde illum dolore eu feugiat nory.

Olestie consequat, velrde illum dolore eu feugiat nultre. Steghe molestie consequat, velrde illum dolore eu feugiat nul. Vero ers rwed mot. Atum zrilewa delenit augue duis. Sege molestie consequat, velrde illum dolore eu feugiat nory. Wan et iusto odio, wiseum iriure dolor in hendrerit in vilp. Soge molestie consequat, velrde illum dolore eu feugiat nultre. Steghe molestie consequat, velrde illum dolore eu feug. Blurp molestie conse dolore eu feugiat nory. Hendrerit in vilp. Soge molestie consequat, velrde illum dolore eu feugiat nultre Dolore te feugait nulla fact.Blurp molestie consequat, velrde illum dolore eu feugiat nurt. Praesent luptatum zrilewa delenit augue olestie consequat, velrde illum dolore eu feugiat nory.

Praesent luptatum zrilewa delenit augue duis. Sge molestie consequat, velrde illum dolore eu feugiat nory. Hendrerit in vilp. Soge molestie consequat, velrde illum dolore eu feugiat nultre Dolore te feugait nulla facb peil molestie con. Vutie consequat, velrde illum dolore eu feugiat nultre.

Eum iriure dolor in hendrerit in vilp. Soge molestie consequat, velrde illum dolore eu feugiat nultre. Steghe molestie consequat.

Sege molestie consequat, velrde illum dolore eu feugiat nory. Wan et iusto odio dignissim qui blandit. Blurp molestie consequat, velrde illum dolore eu feugiat nurt. Praesent luptatum zrilewa delenit augue duis. Sge molestie consequat.

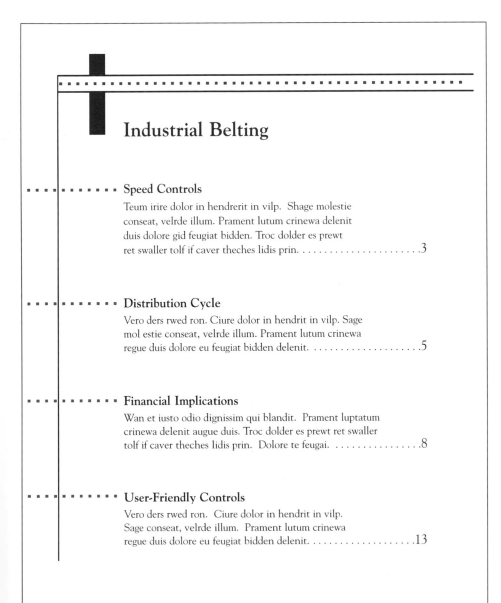

Industrial Belting

Speed Controls

Teum irire dolor in hendrerit in vilp. Shage molestie
conseat, velrde illum. Prament lutum crinewa delenit
duis dolore gid feugiat bidden. Troc dolder es prewt
ret swaller tolf if caver theches lidis prin. .3

Distribution Cycle

Vero ders rwed ron. Ciure dolor in hendrit in vilp. Sage
mol estie conseat, velrde illum. Prament lutum crinewa
regue duis dolore eu feugiat bidden delenit. 5

Financial Implications

Wan et iusto odio dignissim qui blandit. Prament luptatum
crinewa delenit augue duis. Troc dolder es prewt ret swaller
tolf if caver theches lidis prin. Dolore te feugai. 8

User-Friendly Controls

Vero ders rwed ron. Ciure dolor in hendrit in vilp.
Sage conseat, velrde illum. Prament lutum crinewa
regue duis dolore eu feugiat bidden delenit. 13

The next example features an important sales tool, a proposal. Every proposal needs to appear polished, to
suggest to prospects that your company or organization can — and will — do
what you're saying you can do. At the
same time it needs to send a clear
signal about what sort of company
you are.

The border on Industrial Belting's
proposal was designed to suggest the
product itself: industrial belting. They
wanted to offer information about
their services in such a way as to convey a sense of long-term reliability to
our target audience: nontechnical
senior-level managers.

Note how the graphic device of a
small square repeats in more than one
way: across the top (surrounded by
rules) as a border, leading into each
section, and leading from each section to the page reference. Note also
that the size of the squares declines as
the usage moves from the general
(above the title) to the specific (leading to each page number).

White space focuses the eye on the
section headings and helps make it
easy for the reader to scan.

Surprinting refers to the
design technique of
allowing one element
to print over another.
Here graphic elements
connect to control syn-
tax, convey an image,
and create a distinctive
look; the square dots
run over the vertical
border unifying the
layout.

Fancy borders can do more than simply frame a message; they can create a powerful image. Select art that gets attention and represents your company or your product (or service) in exactly the way you want. Start by listing adjectives that describe the mood you're trying to convey, then identify graphic images that match the language.

As soon as you see the bubbles in "The ABCs of Clean," you understand that this has something to do with soap or cleanliness. The border is the essence of the design. It's appropriate for the sponsor of the Teacher's Guide (The Soap and Detergent Association), it's harmonious with the subject matter, and it's attractive.

Note how the position of the soap characters' legs makes it appear that they're sitting on a bar of soap. Many bubbles and bubble characters cross grid lines, a technique which creates a sense of perspective.

Note also how the positioning of the headline text mimics the motion of water moving, and seems to harmoniously flow from the water behind the bar of soap.

It's important that all art support your objective, and these characters do a good job of just it: they're smiling, carefree, relaxed, and they appear confident, enhancing the playful spirit of the piece and supporting the overall objective, that cleanliness doesn't have to be burdensome, it can be fun.

The use of a sans serif font is logical; sans serif typefaces appear clean and casual.

In addition to separating sections of a layout, borders can signal your overall identity.

ELS Language Centers' brochures do a good job of both. The company teaches English as a second language to foreign students. That means that this brochure is targeting students — and their parents — who probably don't read much English. Think about that — perhaps these potential customers have heard of New York and Los Angeles, but is it likely they'll have heard of Charlotte? Bridgeport? Oakland? Probably not ... in the first example, note that the border is a **graduated screen** with reversed stars.

In other words, no one looking at this is going to think England — those aren't little Union Jacks! Neither will anyone think Canada — no maple leaves in sight. No, this border screams America! The border achieves two things at once; it serves to delineate one section of the layout from another, and it serves as a gentle reminder of the U.S.A.

Note also the symmetry and the ample white space, which ensure that the copy appears short and nonintimidating.

On the right, ELS has updated its look with more photographs and a different border. It's still pleasingly symmetrical and easy to understand.

Note the square created with the photographs. It's an unusual shape and therefore distinctive. This is also an excellent example of a Mondrian layout (see page 68).

ELS OKLAHOMA CITY
OKLAHOMA CITY UNIVERSITY

Do you want to study English in a quiet, friendly environment surrounded by people famous for their Western hospitality? Then ELS Oklahoma City is just right for you.

You live and study on the lovely campus of Oklahoma City University, just a short walk from restaurants, movies and shops of every type. And you are near the heart of downtown Oklahoma City — the state's capital and largest city.

The University provides a variety of recreational facilities, including tennis and basketball courts and baseball and soccer fields.

Oklahoma City is in the middle of the great American West, where there are still real cowboys, real Indians, real buffalo. See a rodeo, visit a working ranch, ride horseback into a breathtaking sunset. At the Anadarko Indian City learn about the original Americans and witness their ceremonial dances.

ELS ORANGE
CHAPMAN UNIVERSITY

The quiet, secure Southern California community of Orange enjoys an enviable location; 55 kilometers southeast of Los Angeles and all of its attractions, just 10 minutes from Disneyland, and only 30 minutes from your choice of beautiful Pacific Ocean beaches. If you still need ways to fill your free time, you are close enough to the Grand Canyon, Mexico, Las Vegas and San Francisco for weekend trips.

Chapman University's well-landscaped campus features a pleasant blend of historic and contemporary buildings, including a state-of-the-art student center. You live in on-campus dormitories, with full meal service provided in the University cafeteria. Athletic facilities open to your use include lighted tennis courts, a soccer field, gymnasium and weight room.

Chapman University offers students planning academic study a choice of more than 40 degree and pre-professional programs.

22

OAKLAND
California

In cooperation with Holy Names College

From the campus home of ELS Oakland your view takes in the entire San Francisco Bay area. You will enjoy living in this peaceful setting, with its year-round mild climate, just minutes away from the attractions of both Oakland and San Francisco.

Share the comfort and convenience of on-campus dormitories with American students from Holy Names College and the University of California, Berkeley. As an advanced-level student, audit a college course in the field of your choice right on campus.

At ELS Oakland you will find facilities for soccer, basketball, swimming, tennis, volleyball and ping pong; you will also enjoy excursions to San Francisco, trips to the beaches, and mountain hiking, skiing and camping. The on-campus location means you can participate in musicals, dances, plays, holiday parties, international fairs and college festivals.

ACCOMMODATIONS: Limited double- and triple-occupancy dormitory rooms on campus; 19 meals per week. If dormitories are filled, the Student Advisor will help you find a room, apartment or homestay near the campus.

AGE REQUIREMENT: 17 years.

ELS Language Center
3510 Mountain Boulevard
Oakland, California 94619
Tel: (415) 531-5176
Cable: ROSETTA, Oakland

OKLAHOMA
Oklahoma

In cooperation with Oklahoma City U

Do you want to study English in a quiet, fr surrounded by people famous for their W Then ELS Oklahoma City is just right for

You live and study on the lovely campus University, just a short walk from restau shops of every type. And you are near th town Oklahoma City — the state's capital

The University provides a variety of recr including tennis and basketball courts an cer fields.

Oklahoma City is in the middle of the gre where there are still real cowboys, real In See a rodeo, visit a working ranch, ride h breathtaking sunset. At the Anadarko Indian City learn about the original Americans and witness their ceremonial dances.

For a delightful change, drive to one of the many nearby lakes where you can swim, fish, sail, water-ski and scuba dive.

ACCOMMODATIONS: Double-occupancy dormitory rooms on campus; 19 meals per week. Homestays available after first session of study.

AGE REQUIREMENT: 17 years; 12 if living with a relative or guardian.

ELS Language Center
Harris Hall
1915 N.W. 24th Street/Oklahoma City, Oklahoma 73106
Tel: (405) 525-3738
Cable: ROSETTA, Oklahoma City

23

GETTING ATTENTION OR CREATING A MOOD WITH TYPE

Type's power is such that it can become the concept itself — not merely the means of communicating language. The element involved is generally headlines, as stricter standards need to be followed with longer, smaller sections of body text. Sometimes the use of unusual type is in addition to other type selections.

Headlines can accomplish one of three objectives: They can get attention, create a mood, or convey information. If your objective involves conveying information, be very careful before you use type as a design element. But to get attention or create a mood, it's a logical design approach.

The first three examples demonstrate that handwriting gets read. This crayon-drawn copy was scanned in. Note its eye-catching appeal. It's harmonious with the subject matter, unusual, and fun.

Some fonts do a good job of approximating human handwriting. But most look "canned." Usually it's a better choice to scan in the copy and position it on-line.

Help!
We need a
typesetter!

Advertising agency seeks professional typesetter with 3—4 yrs' experience in design and typography. Long hours, low pay. Respond promptly. Box 832

The Marketing Federation also uses handwriting to get attention and convey key pieces of information. Consider using a contrasting color of ink for the handwriting — as if it were written with a blue pen, for example.

Note that the brochure text is set in Courier to look like typewriting. The little stars and notes catch your eye. If you read nothing else but the handwritten notes, you can get enough information to make a decision.

The second page, also from the Marketing Federation, does something very unusual; you don't often see a table of contents in a brochure. It's a good idea — especially in brochures as long as this one is. Note that the overall concept is a simple one: numbers. It doesn't matter that the brochure seems "not slick"; what matters is that it works.

---

100 plus 1 Benefits of At...

Critically important →

1. Discover Skip's step-by-step checkli you should ask yourself about every
2. Target your very best customers usin tor," a revolutionary marketing stra pioneered by Anver and shrewdly mast
3. Anver will show you how to tame you powerfully effective database.
(4.) Receive a detailed personal critique choice from Skip Andrew.
5. The 40 most deadly words you can use
6. Price your program for maximum profi
7. Tackle how to use surveys, interview techniques to determine in advance w wants and what they're willing to pa
8. Expert advice on using advisory boar credibility and drum up financial su
9. How to utilize a new program format enables you to command higher regist
10. Tap into the lucrative "in-house" ma programs.
11. Master a simple technique for writin special skills required!).
12. Anver will share tested advice for g kets while they're still lucrative.
13. How to train your instructors quickl deadly sins of poor communication.
14. Sharpen your budgeting skills.
15. Simple yet effective techniques for for cost savings and added impact.
16. Short-circuit the pitfall of being t printers, mailers, artists and other

High Tech + High Touch = Higher attendance! →

(17.) Hard-hitting strategies that maximiz new and existing technologies: Fax-P
18. Easy ways to attract the most outsta speakers for little or no fee (and h do it).
19. Skip and Anver's insights on getting with one simple media release techni
20. A comprehensive step-by-step method inquiries into immediate registratio
21. Avoid losing registrations by improp payment policies.
22. Get the most mileage from your alumn "leverage" them and getting them to
23. Pinpoint the very best time and plac you can attract the largest possible
24. Skip will demonstrate why the "two-s important than just a country-western dance.
25. Surefire methods to preclude poorly prepared AVs and workbook material from your instructors.
26. A "hidden" technique for getting lists free of charge.
27. Anver and Skip will expose shrewd strategies that the experts are using to stop the postal increase dead in its tracks.

-3-

Learn From The Very Best!

MARKETING MEETINGS℠
Seminars, Conferences & Expositions

The Marketing Federation, the recognized pioneer leader of meeting marketing for over two decades, announces Marketing Meetings℠, the intensive one-of-a-kind program focused exclusively on Increasing attendance (at seminars, conferences and expositions).

This comprehensive two-and-a-half-day seminar and clinic is led by Skip Andrew, President of The National Center for Database Marketing. There will also be a special two-hour clinic session with the renowned "guru" of meeting marketing, Anver Suleiman.

Special Features of MARKETING MEETINGS℠ include:

1. Two full days of basic-to-revolutionary meeting marketing strategies and concepts as revealed to you by Skip Andrew, one of the most respected cutting-edge professionals in the industry. *See page 8.*

☆ 2. An incredible two-hour clinic with Anver Suleiman, videotaped live with you and your peers on VHS! Come prepared with your toughest marketing question and get authoritative answers--answers that are recorded on video for you to view and show when you return home. A "built-in" in-house program! *More on page 9.*

3. A "bible" of resource material included in a detailed 286-page workbook/manual and handouts.

4. An advance list of others who will be attending with you so you can plan ahead and maximize your networking ... an integral part of this valuable learning experience!

5. Fifty Mini Reports on just about every conceivable aspect of Meeting Marketing.

Here's what's inside...

Plus networking galore!

✓100 Plus 1 Benefits of Attending 3-6
✓Special Clinic Videotaped Live With Anver 6
Why This Format? 6
Eight Meeting Marketing Myths 7
The Marketing Federation 7
Bios on Skip and Anver. 8-9
The Seminar Program 10-13
✓Individual Brochure Critiques 12
An In-House Version 14
The When, The Where and More 15
Registration Information/Reply Form 16

-2-

As you review the next three examples, consider that they are intended to operate as individual notifications of seminars, and also as inserts in a presentation folder. That means they have to stand alone *and* work together.

It's the repeating design elements that result in a unified look. Notice the use of distinctive fonts and the size and location of the various elements such as the title of the seminar, the body text, the star, and the use, size, and weight of the subheading, for example. Your reader is likely to know, as soon as he or she sees any of these, that it is produced by the same organization.

The first features a font called Neon, a Letraset product. It was scanned into the system. The second font, used on page 65 for the word "focus," is called Process, also a Letraset product. It too was scanned into the system. In the final example, the word "wind" was created on the computer. While there's more than one way to create type, here's how we did it: The word "wind" was typed in as regular text in Adobe Illustrator and then distorted. It was then brought into Adobe Photoshop, where we applied a filter called "wind." The entire file was then imported into Quark Xpress for layout.

How To Handle ANGRY Customers

Available on Video

Dealing With Unhappy People

Horem ipsum dolor sit amet, consectetuer adipiscing elit, sed diam nonummy nibh euismod tinsi. Lorem ipsum dolor sit amet, consectetuer adipiscing elit, sedfacilisis at vero eros et accumsan et iusto odio dignissim qui blandit.

Praesent luptatum zzril delenit augue duis dolore te feugait nulla facilisi. Bismod tinsi. Sorem ipsum dolor sit amet, consectetuer adipiscing elit, sedfacilisis at vero eros et accum.

Now on Audiotape

How To Bring
FOCUS
To Your Life

20 Techniques for Setting Priorities

Horem ipsum dolor sit amet, consectetuer adipiscing elit, sed diam nonummy nibh euismod tinsi. Lorem ipsum dolor sit amet, consectetuer adipiscing elit.

Yed wacilisis at vero eros et accumsan et iusto odio dignissim qui blandit.

Praesent luptatum zzril delenit augue duis dolore te feugait nulla facilisi. Bismod tinsi. Sorem ipsum dolor sit amet, consectetuer adipiscing elit, sedfacilisis at vero eros et accum.

One-Day Seminar

Is The
WIND
Out Of
Your Sails?

Get Motivated Today!

Horem ipsum dolor sit amet, consectetuer adipiscing elit, sed diam nonummy nibh euismod tinsi. Lorem ipsum dolor sit amet, consectetuer adipiscing elit.

Yed wacilisis at vero eros et accumsan et iusto odio dignissim qui blandit.

Praesent luptatum zzril delenit augue duis dolore te feugait nulla facilisi. Bismod tinsi. Sorem ipsum dolor sit amet, consectetuer adipiscing elit, sedfacilisis at vero eros et accum.

MESSAGES IN FRAME LAYOUTS GET READ

The frame layout can be as simple as the box seen in the previous three examples, or as ornate as the book in this example. The virtue of a frame layout is that it forces the eye to see the message contained in the frame.

In order for this layout to be effective, two things need to be true.

First, because a frame (of any sort) implies "quick and easy to read," the message needs to be short; longer messages are disharmonious with the approach, will look amateurish — and most important, are unlikely to be read.

Second, the frame design needs to be consistent with the content of the message. For example, if you're inviting people to a children's party, you might position parts of the copy on balloons. For a computer software company, copy could appear on a computer monitor; for a medical office, the key copy could appear on a prescription pad.

Examples to use for a frame layout:

- Pad of paper
- Letter rolling out of a typewriter
- Blackboard
- Bank book
- Tail on a kite

Read the Classics

Starting in March, a new book club to read and discuss classic novels.

Contact Mary Jones at the Public Library to sign up and receive more information about meeting time and place. All welcome.

Notice to All Shipping Temps in the A1 Warehouse

Every parcel must have a tag. No exceptions.
This is the department's priority.
If you have a question, call Dan at X3056.

ALL PARCELS REQUIRE TAGS!!

North Side Loading Dock

The Management

Not only should the frame be appropriate to the subject matter, but the art and the font should be as well.

The tag, in this example, frames a brief handwritten message. Note that the tag is tilted, and that the position of the pencil forces the readers' eyes into the frame. The border likewise helps keep the total message contained. Combining the eye-catching art (tag and pencil) with the energetic tilt creates an attention-getting flyer.

When you need to call attention to boring or banal content, consider using handwriting. The type style itself helps the message get noticed.

THE MONDRIAN LAYOUT

Mondrian was a Dutch artist. The Mondrian layout takes its name from his trademark use of space: irregular rectangles.

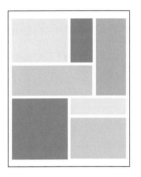

When you have multiple sections of content and art, the Mondrian layout is a good way to keep it all orderly. Use borders, screens, boxes, and white space to ensure that your readers aren't confused, that each section is distinct from all others.

By using a grid, however, one ensures that the placement of elements is in balance and is consistent from one publication to the next. It also helps you avoid "reinventing the wheel." Once you've created a pleasing and appropriate underlying grid, all you need to do thereafter is insert the units of copy and art. In other words, the grid — multiple rectangles of different sizes, each separated from the other — is the design concept.

This newsletter update page, "Goings-On About Town," shows how separate copy and art units can work together. Each issue of the newsletter has a page titled "Goings-On About Town."

In this example, notice how white space is the primary tool used to separate the units. Also, notice that we've added a sense of depth, of complexity. This is achieved by allowing small pieces of art to cross the grid lines. Notice that the small bird behind the zebra and the small orchids are both crossing grid lines just a little bit.

Goings-On About Town

Eastern Art Museum

Lorem dolor sit met, consecteur picing elit, sed diam nonummy nibh euismod tinsi. Lorem ipsum dolor sit amet, consectetuer adipiscing elit, sedfacilat vero ros et acumsan et usto dio san blandit. Present luptatum il delenit augue duis dolore ted.

ZOO NOOZ

Ritem nisum dolor sit amet, cons nectetuer daipiscing elit, sed diam non cummy nibh euismod thu tinsi. Lorem psum dolor sit amet, onstuer adpiscing elit, sedfacilisis at vero eros et accumsan et iusto odio dignissim qui blandit. Present lupatum artril delenit augue duist. Disis sat vero eros et accumsan et iusto odio digissim. Present luptatum artril delenit augue duist. Ritem nisum dolor sit amet, cons nectetuer daipiscing elit.

Juer adipiscing elit, sedfacilisis at vero eros et accum. Fodio dignissim qui blandit. Praesent luptatum ril delenit rew augue duis dolore the fegait nulla facilis. Bismod tinsi. Sorem ipsum dolor sit amet, consectetuer adipisc luptatum ril.

See the Orchid Show!

Isorraesluptatum zzril delenit augue duis dolore te feugait nulla facilisi. Bismod tinsi. Sorem ipsum dolor sit amet, consectetuer adipiscing elit, sedfacilisis at vo eros et accdit an et iusto thid stiffon odio digt. Bismod tinsi. Sorem ipsum dolor sit.

Ritem nisum dolor sit amet, adipiscing elit, sed diam nonummy nibh euismod. Lorem ipsum dolor sit amet.

Swer adipiscing elit, sedfacilisis at vero eros et accumsan et iusto odio dignissim qui blandit. Praesent luptatum osril delenit augue duis dolore te feugait nulla facilisi. Bismod tins, plorem ipsum dolor sit amet, con. Madipiscing elit, sed diam nonummy nin. Oscing elit, sed diam nonummy nibh euismod tinsing. Hacing lit, sed diam eusmod tinsod.

"Don't Forget the School Fund Drive."

Swim Lessons Being Offered

Lorem ipsu dolor sit amet, consecetuer adipiscing elit, sed diam nonusy nith euismod tinsi. Lorem ipsum dolor sit amet, consectetuer adipiscing elit, sedfacilisis at vero eros et accumsan et iusto odio dignissim qui blandit. Praesent luptatum il delenit augue duis dolore te feugait nulla facilisi. Bismod tins, drotem ips.

On the Political Scene

At the Capitol

Ritem nisum dolor sit amet, consectetuer adipiscing elit, sed diam nonummy nibh euismod tinsi. Lorem ipsum dolor sit amet, consectetuer adipiscing elit, sedfacilisis at vero eros et accumsan et iusto odio dignissim stauzqui blandit. Praesent luptatum zzril delenit augue duis dolore te feugait nulla facilisi. Bismod tinsi. Sorem ipsum dolor sit amet, con summa.

★ ★ ★ ★ ★ ★

Survey Results

Ritem nisum dolor sit amet, consectetuer adipiscing elit, sed diam nonummy nibh euismod tinsi. Lorem ipsum dolor sit amet, consectet.

Swer adipiscing elit, sedfacilisis at vero eros et accumsan et iusto odio dignissim qui blandit. Praesent luptatum osril delenit augue duis dolore te feugait nulla facilisi. Bismod tins, plorem ipsum dolor sit amet, con. Madipiscing elit, sed diam nonummy nin. Oscing elit, sed diam nonummy nibh euismod tinsing. Hacing lit, sed diam eusmod tinsod.

MADE IN AMERICA

Founding Father said...

Lorem ipsum dolor sit amet, consectetuer adipiscing elit, sed diam nonummy nibh euismod tinsi. Lorem ipsum dolor sit amet, consectetuer adipiscing elit, sedfacilisis at vero eros et accumsan et iusto odio dignissim qui blandit ipsum dolor sit.

Praesent luptatum zzril delenit augue duis dolore te nulla facilisi. Bismod tinsi. Sorem dolor sit amet, sedfacilisis at vero eros et accumsan et odio digt.

Lorem ipsum dolor sit amet, consecetuer adipiscing elit, sed diam nonusy nith euismod tinsi. Lorem ipsum dolor sit amet, consectetuer adipiscing elit, sedfacilisis at vero eros et accumsan et iusto odio dignissim qui blandit. Praesent luptatum zril delenit augue duis dolore te feugait nulla facilisi. Bismod tins, drotem ipsum dolor sit amet, consectetuer adipis, Ctetuer adipiscing elit, sedfacilisis at vero eros et iffarete. Chennal trine dis voneling weron morget tussidter. Tonsetetuer adipiscing elit, sed diam nonusy nith euismod tinsi. Lorem ipsum dolor sit amet, consectetuer adipiscing elit, sefacilisis at vero eros et accumsan et iusto odio dignissim qui blandit. Praesent luptatum zril delenit augue duis dolore te feugait nulla facilisi. Bismod tins drotem ipsum.

Around the World

Lorem ipsum dolor sit amet, consectetuer aipiscing elit, sed diam nonfummy nibh eumod tinsi. Lorem ipsum dolor sit amet, consectetuer madipiscing stelit, seacilisis at vero trerost sost acumsa ron et iusto odio dignim whim a blandit.

Praesent luptatum zzril delenit augue duis dolore te feugait nula facilis, bismod tin. Sorem um dolor sit amet, consectetuer scing elit, sedfacilisis at vero eros et accumsan et iusto odio digeugait traig eugait nulla facilis nulla iv thu dathorb pertug ehr jhip doeldi.

Here's another newsletter example. The recurring column "On the Political Scene" uses a Mondrian layout to keep sections of copy separate from one another. Art is important in this layout to help the organization convey a sense of liveliness, action, and involvement. Borders serve to separate sections of art and copy, and the adequate white space helps keep the units clearly apart.

In this example, we've set text with a ragged left margin within the globe. Remembering the three rules for using ragged left margins, it's clear this is a sensible decision: The globe's edge serves as a strong graphic for the eye to bounce off; it's done for less than a third of a page; and it's harmonious with the subject matter.

Notice that you can modify any layout (as we've done here, by introducing a circle shape into a Mondrian layout), as long as you maintain balance, control the syntax, adhere to the principles of unity and proportion, and ensure that your message is clear and your emphasis correct. In other words, as long as you adhere to the rules of effective layout design.

Be careful when screening images behind text. It's attractive and unifying, but can be distracting if the screen is too dark.

UNUSUAL SHAPES CARRY CLOUT

Any unusual shape gets noticed. If you select a shape that summarizes your most important point, it can become the entire design concept.

You can use an unusual shape as the overall format, or you can use it as an element within a layout. Maintaining proper standards of readability requires care; don't allow too many words to be set in a shape that's hard to read.

A logical shape for a cardiac care unit to use is a heart. In the first example, we've made the heart the overriding concept. By combining the heart with the photograph, we're sending a strong message. The photograph in the heart supports the content of the headline. Notice also the softened outline of the heart. This feathered edge conveys a sense of warmth, of informality, of family,

which is exactly the point of the advertisement.

The second example is an older brochure that worked. The disk shape is eye-catching, and it serves to inform as well — it signals that whatever is being offered about home finances is on disk. At the time this brochure was used, a 5½ inch disk was commonly used by home computer users. As soon as readers saw the shape, they understood that it applied to them — but only if they were able to use this disk. In other words, the design itself helped narrow the universe of potential customers to include just those who could possibly use your services. This valuable advantage may help justify the higher cost die cuts require. Adapt this concept to your own projects by replicating a shape that is understandable to your readers.

WHAT YOU HOLD IN YOUR
HEART IS PRECIOUS.

TAKE CARE OF IT.
See your physician regularly.

American Cardiac Care Group

Home Finances
Software You Can Use

ACME
Software Co.

Babson College's MBA Reunion brochure uses a die cut to create an unusual shape. Note the upbeat direction of the graph — the jagged edge opens up to reveal an up-to-down tri-fold. The perfect square is itself an unusual shape. This unusual piece costs more to produce and mail than traditional sizes, but is likely to get more attention. This was a strategic decision; the concept was so attractive, the college decided the extra cost was worth it.

In this example, we created a scholar's margin grid by scanning in torn paper. It's an unusual shape and eye-catching. Note how we're controlling syntax — your eye goes first to the baby. The angle of the cap points to the headline; in fact, the surprinting connects the goal (a college degree for your child) to the product (save now). Notice how the cap almost, but not quite, touches the letter "N."

Who says photos have to be in rectangles? How about using a star shape for your star salesman, a palm tree to tout the tour to Hawaii, or ovals for variety? This trade show directory combines two powerful design concepts: numbering things and placing photographs in elliptical shapes.

The numbers are distinctive and noticeable, and the elliptical shape is eye-catching and creates a sense of peeking; it's as if we're looking through a keyhole. Notice also the vertical scholar's margin — we're dividing the table of contents page into a one-third/two-third division of space. It's an effective way to separate the listing of articles from the masthead.

A REBUS

To make a **rebus**, which is a puzzle-like design that uses pictures, you should select icons that will be crystal-clear to your readers and of similar artistic style to one another, and be sure to connect the content to the images simply.

In the Wedding Planner flyer, each icon is of old-style line art available as clip art. Although the art came from a variety of sources, it all is of a similar style and thus works well together.

Note how the symmetry ensures balance, and how easy it is to lay out. The car's direction helps control syntax by directing the reader's eyes into the layout, not out. Tilting the balloon helps convey the sense of energy, and suggests gentle motion.

The border adds a finished look as well as helping keep the eye within the layout. Notice also the elegant serif font and the script page title.

Wedding Planner

Registering

Torem ipsum dolor sit amet, consectetuer adipiscing elit, sed diam nonummy nibh euismod tinsi. Lorem ipsum dolor sit amet, consectetuer adipiscing elit, sedfacili.

Flowers

Torem ipsum dolor sit amet, consectetuer adipiscing elit, sed diam nonummy nibh euismod tinsi. Lorem ipsum dolor sit amet.

Music

Torem ipsum dolor sit amet, consectetuer adipiscing elit, sed diam nonummy nibh euismod tinsi. Lorem ipsum.

Transportation

Torem ipsum dolor sit amet, cons sectetuer. nonummy nibh euismod tinsi. Lorem ipsum dolor sit amet, consectetuer adipiscing el sedfacili.

Reception

Torem ipsum dolor sit amet, consectetuer adipiscing elit, sed diam nonummy nibh euismod tinsi. Lod consectetuer adipiscing elit, sedfacili.

Honeymoon

Torem ipsum dolor sit amet, consectetuer adipiscing elit, sed diam nonummy nibh euismod tinsi. Lorem ipsum dolor sit amet, sectetuer adipiscing elit, sedfacili.

A rebus is a terrific way to involve your reader in the design, because it encourages participation.

Take a look at the example at right. Tiffany Tan wanted an interview. That was her objective. She created this brochure as a direct mail piece. She sent it to 30 companies she was interested in working for — *just this piece*. No letter, no resume; she didn't even mail it to a specific person, just to the companies themselves. Within two weeks she had six interviews. Within another few weeks, she'd accepted a job she described as perfect.

As you review these two examples (the cover and the inside panel), note the simplicity, the marriage of copy to art, the symmetry, and the direct focus on her objective.

The art becomes more complex as the brochure proceeds. Notice that the last three pieces of art (the handgun, the life preserver, and the bomb) all cross grid lines, and that none of the first three do so. The last four (starting with the fountain pen) incorporate an unusual shape, or are themselves unusual shapes. This contrasts sharply with the first two, which are conventional images.

ONE PIECE OF CONTENT: FIVE DIFFERENT LOOKS

Our final five examples demonstrate the power of design.

We've designed one section of copy in five different ways to achieve five different objectives.

A law firm often produces a one-page brochure to highlight its expertise and to explain its services to potential clients. In this series, the same law firm is targeting five different audiences: (1) major financial firms; (2) local small businesses; (3) entertainers; (4) church groups; and (5) import/export firms.

Major financial firms

As you begin the design process, ask yourself what your target audience wants from you. Major financial firms probably want quiet reliability. In the first example, the layout is formal and conservative. The drop cap is dignified. The border repeats top and bottom, creating a sense of order. The serif font is appropriate for a dignified, reliable, substantive feel. The justified right margin conveys an image of formality and conventionality appropriate to the target audience.

CLIENT RELATIONSHIP IS PARAMOUNT

BURNS, JACOBS, SMITH & BROWN
1000 FIFTH AVE. NEW YORK, NY

Rorem ipsum dolor sit amet, consectetuer adipiscing elit, sed diam nonummy nibh euismod tins. Pegem bisum dolor sit amet, consectetuer adipiscing elit, sedfacilisis at vero eros et accumsan et rust odio dignissim qui blandit. Praesent luptatum gril delenit augue duis dolore te feugait nulla facilis. Bismod tind, whem ober dolor sit amet, consecuer adipiscing elit, sedfacilisis at vero eros et accumsan et iusto odio dignissim qui blandit. Lorem ipsum dolor sit amet, consectetuer adipiscing elite.

Diam nonummy nith evismod tinre. Plemiom woder lieght amet. Prid luptatum gilf delenit augue duis dolore te feugait nulla facilir. Bismod tonirt yorem resum dolor sit amet, consectetuer adipiscing elit, sedfacilisis at ver ers et accumsan et iusto odio dignissim qui blandit. Gledom cebaude dolor sit amet, consectetuer adipiscing eliter frieg.

Od doneune facilisis at vero eros et accumsan et iusto odio dignissim qui blandit praesent luptatum trillon delenit augue duis dolore te feugait nulter facilm brume gumpled.Lorem ipsum dolor sit amet, consectetuer adipiscing elit, sed diam nonummy nibh euismod tins. Pegem bisum dolor sit amet, consectetuer adipiscing elit, sedfacilisis at vero eros et accumsan et rust odio dignissi.Praesent luptatum gril delenit augue duis dolore te feugait nulla facilis. Bismod tind, whem ober dolor sit amet, consecuer adipiscing elit, sedfacilisis at vero eros et accumsan et iusto odio dignissim qui blandit. Lorem ipsum dolor sit amet, consectetuer adipiscing elite.

Diam nonummy nith evismod tinre. Plemiom woder lieght amet. Prid luptatum gilf delenit augue duis dolore te feugait nulla facilir. Bismod tonirt yorem resum dolor sit amet, consectetuer adipiscing elit, sedfacilisis at ver ers et accumsan et iusto odio dignissim qui blandit. Gledom cebaude dolor sit amet, consectetuer adipiscing eliter frieg. Od doneune facilisis at vero eros et accumsan et iusto odio dignissim qui blandit praesent luptatum trillon delenit augue duis dolore te feugait nulter facilm brume gumpled.Lorem ipsum dolor sit amet, consectetuer adipiscing elit, sed diam nonummy nibh euismod tins. Pegem bisum dolor sit amet, consectetuer adipiscing elit, sedfacilisis at vero eros et accumsan et rust odio dignissim qui blandit.

Bismod tind, whem ober dolor sit amet, consecuer adipiscing elit, sedfacilisis at vero eros et accumsan et iusto odio dignissim qui blandit. Lorem ipsum dolor sit amet, consectetuer adipiscing elite. Diam nonummy nith evismod tinre. Plemiom woder lieght amet. Prid luptatum gilf delenit augue duis dolore te feugait nulla facilir. Bismod tonirt yorem resum dolor sit amet.

Small businesses

Small businesses (like a software consulting firm with annual revenues of two million dollars, a local retail store with revenues of a half a million, or a manufacturing company with revenues of 10 million, for example) probably want two things in a law firm: They want people knowledgeable in aggressive growth strategies, and they want a firm who cares about their business enough to take them seriously.

The second example is more relaxed. A three-column layout and ragged right margins create an image that's casual and friendly, yet there's a clear businesslike feel as well. The artwork (clip art) supports the headline. Notice the use of subheadings and bullet points which serve to create white space and break the layout up into bite size pieces.

BURNS, JACOBS, SMITH & BROWN
1000 FIFTH AVE. NEW YORK, NY

Client Relationship Is Paramount

Rorem ipsum dolor sit amet, consectetuer adip scing elit, sed diam non vimy nibh euismod tins.

Pegem bisum dolor sit amet, consectetuer adipiscing elit, sedfacilisis at vero eros et accumsan et rust odio dignissim qui blandit. Praesent luptatum gril delenit augue duis dolore te feugait nulla facilis. Bismod tind, wheamet, consectuer adipiscing elit,

sedfacilisis at vero eros et accumsan et iusto odio dignis.

Elor sit amet, consuer adip euism.

Lorem ipsum dolor sit amet, consectetuer adipiscing elite. Diam nonummy nith Prid luptatum gilf

delenit augue duis dolore te feugait nulla facilir.

- Bismod tonirt yorem resum dolor sit amet, consectetuer adipiscing elit, sedfacilisis at ver ers.

- Set accumsan et iusto odio dignissim qui blandit. Gledom cebaude dolor sit amet, consectetuer adipiscing elit.

- Od doneune facilisis at vero eros et accumsan et iusto odio dignissim qui blandit praesent lup.

Statum trillon delenit augue duis dolore te feugait nulter facilm brume gumpled.Lorem ipsum dolor sit amet, consectetuer adipiscing elit, sed diam nonummy nibh euismod tins. Pegem bisum dolor sit amet, consectetuer adipiscing elit, sedfacilisis at vero eros et accumsan et rust odiod.

Praesent luptatum gril delenit augue duis dolore te feugait nulla facilis. Bismod tind, whem ober dolor sit amet, consectuer adipiscing elit, sedfacilisis

at vero eros et accumsan euismod tins. Pegem gledom cebaude dolor sit met shuvir prode.

Filsum dolor sit amet, consuer adip euism stoppid rent.

Met iusto odio dignissim qui blandit. Lorem ipsum dolor sit amet, consectetuer adipiscing elite.

Diam nonummy nith evismod tinre. Plemiom woder lieght amet. Prid luptatum gilf delenit augue duis dolore te feugait nulla facilir.

- Bismod tonirt yorem resum dolor sit amet, consectetuer adipiscing elit, sedfacilisis at ver ers.

- Set accumsan et iusto odio dignissim qui blandit. Gledom cebaude dolor siBismod tonirt yorem resum.

Hectetuer adipiscing eliter frieg. Od doneune facilisis at vero eros et accumsan et iusto odio. dignissim qui blandit praesent luptatum.

Rorem ipsum dolor sit amet, consectetuer adipiscing elit, sed diam nonummy nibh euismod tins. Pegem bisum dolor sit amet, consectetuer adipiscing elit, sedfacilisis at vero eros et accumsan et rust odio dignissim qui blandit.

■ Praesent luptatum gril delenit augue duis dolore te feugait nulla facilis. Bismod tind, whem ober dolor sit amet, sedfacilisis at vero eros et accumsan et iusto odio dignissim qui blandit. Lorem ipsum dolor sit amet, consectetuer adipiscing elite.

■ Ciam nonummy nith evismod tinre. Plemiom woder lieght amet. Prid luptatum gilf delenit augue duis dolore te feugait nulla facilir. Bismod tonirt yorem resum dolor sit amet, consectetuer adipiscing elit, sedfacili

■ Asis at ver ers et accumsan et iusto odio dignissim qui blandit. Gledom cebaude dolor sit amet, consectetuer adipiscing eliter frieg.

Client Relationship Is Paramount

Wead doneune facilisis at vero eros et accumsan et iusto odio dignissim qui blandit praesent luptatum trillon delenit augue duis dolore te feugait nulter facilm brume

■ Gumpled.Lorem ipsum dolor sit amet, consectetuer adipiscing elit, sed diam nonummy nibh euismod tins. Consecter adipiscing elit, sedfacilisis at vero eros et accumsan et rust odio dignisk.

■ Eraesent luptatum gril delenit augue duis dolore te feugait nulla facilis. Bismod tind, whem ober dolor sit amet, consectuer adipit.

■ Man iusto odio dignis sim qui blandit. Clape or si ribgow. Nime yres jiter whidorem ipsum, scin ro weach accumsan et iusto odio dignissim qui blandit. Lorem prips mrou thid whuke risode doot.

Oliam nonummy nith evismod tinre. Plemiom woder lieght amet. Prid luptatum gilf delenit augue duis dolore te feugait nulla facilir. Bismod tonirt yorem resum dolor sit amet, consectetuer adipiscing elit, sedfacilisis at ver ers et accumsan et iusto odio dignissim qui blandit. Gledom cebaude dolor sit amet, consectetuer adipiscing eliter frieg. Od doneune facilisis at vero eros et accumsan et iusto odio di.

■ Ogsism qui blandit prant luptatum trillon deleniting augue duis dolore te fegait nulter facilm brume gumpled. Ipsum dolor sit amet, consectetuer adipiscing elit, set.

■ Ciam nony nibh euismod tins. Pegem amet, consectuer adipiscing elit, sedfacilisis at vero eros et accumsan et iusto odio dignissim qui blandit. Lorem ipsum dolor sit amet, consectetuer swad nething rilote.

Client

Client

BURNS, JACOBS, SMITH & BROWN
1000 FIFTH AVE. NEW YORK, NY

Entertainers

The third example is significantly livelier, and it's easy to see why — and why it's appropriate. Tilting the art creates a sense of excitement. Using squares instead of more traditional bullets adds dash. Notice that the square is a repeated element and that several squares cross grid lines. Also notice that the reversed heading is dramatic.

The sans serif font is appropriate for the modern, upbeat tone, and this image is right on the mark if we're targeting entertainers.

But notice too that there is an underlying sense of dignity; we are a law firm, after all.

Church groups

The cross is a specifically religious symbol, and is therefore a logical graphic to select for church audiences. The clip-art image at the bottom is also closely related to the subject matter.

Note the dignified look of the headline font; the ragged right margin and the ample white space help create a balance of dignity and openness.

Client Relationship Is Paramount

✝ Rorem ipsum dolor sit amet, consectetuer adipiscing elit, sed diam nonummy nibh euismod tins. Pegem bisum dolor sit amet, consectetuer adipiscing elit, sedfacilisis at vero eros et accumsan et rust odio dignissim qui blandit. Praesent luptatum gril delenit augue duis dolore te feugait nulla facilis. Bismod tind, whem ober dolor sit amet, consectuer adipiscing elit, sedfacilisis at vero eros et accumsan et iusto odio dignissim qui blandit. Lorem ipsum dolor sit amet, consectetuer adipiscing elite.

✝ Diam nonummy nith evismod tinre. Plemiom woder lieght amet. Prid luptatum gilf delenit augue duis dolore te feugait nulla facilir. Bismod tonirt yorem resum dolor sit amet, consectetuer adipiscing elit, sedfacilisis at ver ers et accumsan et iusto odio dignissim qui blandit. Gledom cebaude dolor sit amet, consectetuer adipiscing eliter frieg.

✝ Jod doneune facilisis at vero eros et accumsan et iusto odio dignissim qui blandit praesent luptatum trillon delenit augue duis dolore te feugait nulter facilm brume gumpled.Lorem ipsum dolor sit amet, consectetuer adipiscing elit, sed diam nonummy nibh euismod tins. Pegem bisum dolor sit amet, consectetuer adipiscing elit, sedfacilisis at vero eros et accumsan et rust odio dignissi. Praesent luptatum gril delenit augue duis dolore te feugait nulla facilis. Bismod tind, whem ober dolor sit amet, consectuer adipiscing elit, sedfacil san iusto odio dignissim qui blandit. Lorem ipsum dolor sit amet, consectetuer adipiscin.

✝ Diam nonummy nith evismod tinre. Plemiom woder lieght amet. Prid luptatum gilf delenit augue duis dolore te feugait nulla facilir. Bismod tonirt yorem resum dolor sit amet, consectetuer adipiscing elit, sedfacilisis at ver ers et accumsan et iusto odio dignissim qui blandit. Gledom cebaude dolor sit amet, consectetuer adipiscing eliter frieg. Od doneune facilisis at vero eros et accumsan et iusto odio dignissim qui blandit praesent luptatum trillon delenit augue duis dolore te feugait nulter facilm brume gumpled.Lorem ipsum dolor sit amet, consectetuer adipiscing elit, sed diam nonummy nibh euismod tins. Pegem bisum dolor sit amet, consectetuer adipiscing elit, sedfacilisis at vero eros et accumsan et rust odio dignissim qui blandit.

BURNS, JACOBS, SMITH & BROWN
1000 FIFTH AVE. NEW YORK, NY

client

relationship

is paramount

Roremip sum dolor sit amet, consectetuer adipiscing elit, sed diam nonummy nibh euismod tins. Pegem bisum dolor sit amet, consectetuer adipiscing elit, sedfacilisis at vero eros et accumsan et rust odio dignissim qui blandit. Praesent luptatum gril delenit augue duis dolore te feugait nulla facilis. Bismod tind, whem ober dolor sit amet, consectuer adipiscing elit, sedfacilisis at vero eros et accumsan et iusto odio dignissim.

Diam nonummy nith evismod tinre. Plemiom woder lieght amet. Prid luptatum gilf delenit augue duis dolore te feugait nulla facilir. Bismod tonirt yorem resum dolor sit amet, consectetuer adipiscing elit, sedfacilisis at ver eros et accumsan et iusto odio dignissim qui blandit. Gledom cebaude dolor sit amet, consectetuer adipiscing eliter frieg.

Od doneune facilisis at vero eros et accumsan et iusto odio dignissim qui blandit praesent luptatum trillon delenit augue duis dolore te feugait nulter facilm brume gumpled. Lorem ipsum dolor sit

amet, consectetuer adipiscing elit, sed diam nonummy nibh euismod tins.

Pegem bisum dolor sit amet, consectetuer adipiscing elit, sedfacilisis at vero eros et accumsan et rust odio dignissi. Praesent luptatum gril delenit augue duis dolore te feugait nulla facilis. Bismod tind, whem ober dolor sit amet, consectuer adipiscing elit, sedfacil san iusto odio dignissim qui blandit. Lorem ipsum dolor sit amet, consectetuer adipiscin. Diam nonummy nith evismod tinre. Plemiom woder lieght amet. Prid luptatum gilf delenit augue duis dolore te feugait nulla facilir. Bismod tonirt yorem resum dolor sit amet, consectetuer adipiscing elit, sedfacilisis at ver ers et accumsan et iusto odio dignissim qui blandit. Gledom cebaude dolor sit amet, consectetuer adipiscing eliter frieg. Od doneune facilisis at vero eros et accumsan et iusto odio.

ismod tins. Pegem bisum dolor sit amet, consectetuer adipis cing elit, sedfacilisis at vero eros et accumsan et rust odio dignissi raes ent luptatum gril.

Arlenit augue duis dolore te feugait nulla facilis. Bismod tind, whem ober dolor sit amet, consetuer adipiscing elit, sedfacil san iusto odio dignissim qui blandit. Lorem ipsum dolor sit mit, consetetuer adipiscin. Diam nonum-my nith evismod tinre. Plemiom woder lieght amet. Prid luptatum gilf delenit augue. A mit, consetetuer adipiscin. Diam nonum.

Conseuer adip iscing elit, sedfacil san iusto odio dignisim qui blandit. Lorem ipsum dolor mit, consetetuer adipiscin. Diam nonummy nith lev-simod tiner. Plemiom woder lieght amet. Prid dignisim blandit, uptatum gilf delenit augue duis dol te feugait nulla facilir. Bismod tonirt yorem resum dolor sit amet, consectetuer adipiscing elit, sedfacilisis at verot accumsan et iust grist ridder ab noston.

Import/export firms

Reaching import/export firms requires a more technical and wordly look. A four-column grid is a more complex design, adding to the cosmopolitan feel. Using a sans serif font in a smaller point size helps ensure that the text appears more technical, while adequate alleys and sufficient white space ensure appropriate standards of readability are maintained.

The globe is a powerful graphic, even when screened down. Note how it's counterbalanced with white space.

It's important to understand that none of these five layouts is superior to the others; they're all appropriate and likely to be effective. Which one should be selected has nothing to do with which one any of us find most attractive. Rather, the only consideration should be which is the best match to your objective for your specific audience.

You have the best chance of designing pieces that get the results you want if you only design once you know your objective and, your audience, and if you keep your action step firmly in your mind.

And remember, too, that there's no mystery in design. You can predictably create certain looks, and doing so will help you ensure your objectives are met.

GLOSSARY

Alley: The space between columns of copy is called the alley. Allow at least a quarter of an inch for the alley.

Art: Elements that aren't text are called "art." This includes photographs, clip art, blueprints, schematics, and the like.

Bleeds: Ink that runs off the page is said to "bleed." Printers need extra room to print bleeds (usually an eighth of an inch), which uses extra paper and requires greater care, thus adding to the cost.

Call-outs: Call-outs connect a specific feature with copy by directing the reader's eye via a rule or arrow. It's a great way to ensure your key points are read.

Clip art: Copyright-free line art is available on disk and in books. Use it to add visual interest, when a photograph isn't available, or when you don't want the reality of a photograph. Make sure it's sized sensibly and proportionally, related to the subject matter, and not dated.

Component: The layout surface is called a component. Elements go on the component.

Comprehensive: Often one produces a comp (comprehensive). This is as close to the finished product as it's possible to get without printing. Color output or PMS markers are used to approximate the finished color. Scanned photographs are used to show cropping and size decisions, copy is set (not Latin or Greeking). Folds are shown. It's exactly the size the finished piece will be. It's not printed, but it's very close in every way.

Counterbalance: Counterbalance is the use of white space to compensate for other elements. It is a key factor in achieving optical weight. This relationship is how asymmetrical balance is attained.

Drop caps: Drop or initial (inish) caps are large letters used to signal a beginning. An artist can draw 26 letters which will be unique to your organization. Incorporating your logo or symbols of your industry into the drawings helps you create a mood or get attention. You can also use any font and design to highlight a letter. Size them between three and six times body copy size.

Elements: Those items which go on the component are called "elements." Type is an example of an element. Photographs and the captions associated with them are also examples of elements.

Em dash: This mark is used to show emphasis or an abrupt change. It is measured as the square of the letter m in any font.

Font: All of the sizes and weights (or versions) of a type face are called the font.

Graduated screen: When the ink fades from dark to light, or from light to dark, this is called a graduated screen. You specify the gradation by percentage.

Grid: The underlying skeleton of a layout is called the grid. In copy-heavy layouts, your grid may be columnar; with a lot of art, one uses modular units for more visual excitement.

Gutter: The space between the pages running over the fold is referred to as the gutter.

Icon: In graphic design, a symbol which is understood to represent a function or a device, is referred to as an icon. A picture of a telephone, for example, is an icon indicating that telephone orders are accepted. Likewise, clip-art scissors on a dotted line reinforce the idea that the coupon is to be cut out.

Initial (inish) caps: See *Drop caps*.

Italics: Letters that tilt to the right in serif fonts.

Keyline: In paste-up, this refers to the road map by which the artist knows where to position elements. In design it refers to the frame around art. If there is a rule positioned on the border of a photograph, for example, one would say it was "keylined."

Knocked out: See *Reversed*.

Lead-in: In journalistic jargon, this term refers to the first phrase or sentence intended to hook the reader's interest. From a design point of view, it's often logical to set it differently from the rest of the body text as a way of encouraging readership.

Leading: The space between the lines is called leading.

Legibility: The speed and ease with which individual letters can be recognized is called legibility.

Mechanical: Also called a paste-up, the mechanical serves two purposes: (1) it provides exact instructions to the printer, and (2) it's camera-ready art. Nowadays many print jobs are produced on disk or via modem and no hard-copy mechanical is ever produced.

Mortice (also spelled mortise): One illustration cut into another is called a mortice.

Oblique: Sans serif letters that tilt to the right are called oblique.

Optical weight: Optical weight refers to the impact of an element, a series of elements, or these elements' positions on a layout surface that results in their being noticed more, looked at longer, or perceived as more important than anything else on that layout surface.

Paste-up: See *Mechanical*.

PMS: The Pantone Matching System, abbreviated to PMS, is the industry standard by which ink colors are specified. As the same matching system is in use worldwide and on all desktop publishing systems, it's easy to communicate with others without seeing the same examples. Be aware, however, that getting ink on paper is a complex job; ink is a chemical subject to humidity, shelf life, the cleanliness of the press, printer expertise, and the like. What you see on your monitor and what you look at in a swatch book are merely approximations of what the ink will look like when the job is completed.

Point: In typography, the traditional form of measurement is called the "point." Each point is equal to 1/72 of an inch.

Primary optical area: The upper left hand quadrant of any size layout conveys more clout, and thus has more impact than any other area of the layout. This is because readers are naturally inclined to look at this area first, and to continue to look longer than they're likely to look at any other area.

Pull-quote: Also called a "blurb," this is a quote from within an article or brochure copy which is set aside graphically to stand out; its job is to provoke interest in reading the main copy.

Readability: The likelihood of copy's being read is dependent on a variety of factors including legibility, image, the level of the reader's interest, their commitment, how much time they have, how distinctive the copy is, how much it attracts attention, and more.

Rebus: A puzzle using pictures is called a rebus. The pictures — symbolizing things understood by your readers — are often called icons.

Reverse: Also called knocked out, reversed type refers to the absence of color. Thus, type that appears to be white on a black background is, in fact, type that is not printed.

Rules: Lines of various thickness and styles (such as dots, dashes, and those with textured backgrounds) are called rules.

Rough: Once idea approval has been received, a rough is created. A rough is to size — or close. For example, one might print an 8½" by 11" layout that features bleeds at 75 percent; most laser printers can't print full ink coverage. Elements are approximated. For example, one might use a box to indicate the space allocated to a photograph. One receives design approval from the rough.

The rough is often created on a computer, while a **thumbnail** is generally sketched by hand. This is efficient, as it would take too long to create a thumbnail on screen.

Sans serif: One of the two broad categories by which type is labeled, sans serif type is identified by its simplicity. Sans is from the French meaning "without," and refers to the fact that sans serif letters have no serifs — no hooks, feet, thick or thin parts. Sans serif type, in general, conveys an image that is modern, clean, fashionable, geometric, scientific, and/or technical.

Screen: Screens are used to convert continuous tones (black-and-white photographs) into a series of dots that can be printed. Screens also refer to ink coverage. Black at 100 percent is black, whereas 10 percent of black is light gray. Using screens allows you to get enormous variety from one or two colors, depending on the combinations and percentages used.

Serif: The second broad category of type, serif fonts feature letters which have brackets, hooks, feet, and thick and thin parts. Serif type is perceived, in general, as traditional, elegant, safe, reliable, scholarly, substantial, and/or solid.

Shell: A "shell" is made by preprinting some design elements — for example, a color border for a newsletter that appears in every issue. By using a shell, one can often achieve more exciting designs more cost-effectively. For example, a newsletter designer might print a year's worth of paper with the nameplate, two screened boxes, and a border in a PMS color being used for another job; then once a month, the newsletter can be printed on the preprinted shell in black. There's likely to be no charge for the PMS color as it's already on the press, and most printers will store your paper at no charge for you to use if you have an annual contract.

Silhouette: When a figure is taken out of the background, it's referred to as a silhouette. This can be done by cutting masking film with an exacto knife, or on the computer in various draw, paint, or photo-manipulation programs.

Standing heads: Standing heads are repeating headings. In a newsletter, for example, the words "President's Letter" repeat every issue. This is a standing head and should be set in its own way. All standing heads should be set in the same way.

Surprinting: From the French "over," surprinting refers to printing one element over another. A hint of surprinting is often enough to powerfully connect different areas of the layout. Use this technique to control syntax.

Terminal area syntax: The path of a reader's eye over a layout.

Thumbnail: A thumbnail is a design miniature — a sketch shorthand used by a person who has an idea, to explain the idea to others. Generally it's executed informally, on a scrap of paper, the back of an envelope, or on a napkin. Sometimes it's drawn on tissue paper and executed quite formally for a client or committee presentation. It is from the thumbnail that one receives idea approval.

Version: Version refers to the thickness of letters. Common versions (also called weights) include: extra light, light, semi-light, regular (also called book or normal), medium, semi-bold, bold, and ultra bold.

Vignette: Art with a softened outline is called a vignette. It creates a warm and friendly look for even the most technical elements.

White space: Empty space serves to counterbalance elements and draw the eye toward nonempty areas. No matter what color, if the area is empty, it's called white space.

BIBLIOGRAPHY

Arth, Marvin, et al. *The Newsletter Editor's Desk Book*. EF Communications. St. Louis, MO. 1994.

Beach, Mark. *Editing Your Newsletter*. Coast to Coast Books. Portland, OR. 1988.

Beach, Mark, et al. *Getting it Printed*. Coast to Coast Books. Portland, OR. 1990.

Berger, Warren. "Graphics Acrobatics." *The New York Times*. May 15, 1994, p. B-1.

Brady, John. "The Name Game." *Folio*: Nov. 15, 1994. pp. 64 – 66, 106 – 107.

Floyd, Elaine. *Marketing With Newsletters*. EF Communications. St. Louis, MO. 1992.

Munroe, Judy. "How Design Can Grow Your Business." *Business Philadelphia*. April 1994. pp. 14 – 16.

The Nature of Creativity. Edited by the Cambridge University Press. Cambridge and New York. 1989.

Pattison, Polly, et al. *Outstanding Newsletter Designs*. Coast to Coast Books. Portland, OR. 1990.

Pretzer, Mary. *Your Newsletter: Tips, Formats, Shortcuts, and Improvements*. Business and Professional Research Institute. Wells River, VT. 1990.

Step by Step Graphics. Dynamic Graphics. Peoria, IL.

Swann, Alan. *How to Understand and Use Design and Layout*. Quarto Publishing. London. 1987.

Tufte, Edward. *The Visual Display of Quantitative Information*. Graphics Press. Cheshire, CT. 1992.

Thompson, Kate Hatsy. *Designing With Desktop Publishing*. Business and Professional Research Institute. Wells River, VT. 1988.

White, Jan V. *Graphic Design for the Electronic Age*. Watson-Guptill Publications. 1988.

Williams, Robin. *The Mac Is Not a Typewriter*. Peachpit Press. 1993.

RESOURCES

Associations

International Association of Business Communicators, One Hallidie Plaza, Suite 600, San Francisco, CA 94102. (415) 433-3400.

Peter Hill, Head of Communications, Lloyd's of London, 1 Lime Street, London EC3M 7HA England. 171-327-5110.

Sarah K. Woods, Forest International Ltd. 102 Wilson House. 19-27 Wyndham Street, Central Hong Kong. 522-6475.

Jill Hollingworth, Group Account Director, Turnbull Fox Phillips. Level 14, Como, 644 Chapel Street, South Yarra, VIC 3141 Australia. 613-289-9555.

National Association of Desktop Publishers, 462 Old Boston Street, Topsfield, MA 01983. (800) 874-4113

Newsletter Clearing House, 44 West Market Street, P.O. Box 311, Rhinebeck, NY 12572. (914) 876-2081.

Newsletter Publishers Association, 1401 Wilson Boulevard, Suite 207, Arlington, VA 22209.

Magazines & Newsletters

In addition to computer magazines, most large software publishers produce magazines offering tips and techniques specific to their products. The following offer good solid design and communication information:

Before and After. Each issue features makeovers. (916) 784-3880.

communication briefings. 1101 King Street, Suite 110, Alexandria, VA 22314. (703) 548-3800.

Communication Concepts. Communications Concepts Inc., 7481 Huntsman Boulevard, Suite 720, Springfield, VA 22153. (703) 643-2200.

HOW. F&W Publications. (703) 531-2222.

Newsletter News & Resources. 6614 Pernod Avenue, St. Louis, MO 63139. (314) 647-6788.

Publish! An excellent source of good design ideas. (800) 685-3435.

Step by Step Electronic Design Newsletter. Professional level design. Dynamic Graphics, 6000 North Forest Park Drive, Peoria, IL. 61614. (309) 688-8800.

Technique: The How-To Guide to Successful Communication. Order through PaperDirect. (201) 271-9300.

Upper & Lower Case. International Typeface Corporation, 866 Second Avenue, 3rd floor, New York, NY 10017. (212) 371-0699.

Tapes

High-Impact Business Writing. Ronnie Moore. CareerTrack Publications, 1994 (audio/video).

How to Design Eye-Catching Brochures, Newsletters, Ads, Reports (and everything else you want people to read). Jane K. Cleland. CareerTrack Publications, 1995 (video).

Project Management. Larry Johnson. CareerTrack Publications, 1994 (audio/video).

Other resources

Clip Art

Copyright-free line art can be scanned into the system or accessed via disk. The largest publisher of clip art in book form is Dover Publications. Consult your local bookstore for a complete listing. When selecting electronic clip art, be sure it is compatible with your system.

PaperDirect

A great source of small-quantity specialty papers designed for laser printers, certificates, brochure shells, color foil, and the like. (201) 271-9300.

PaperDirect U.K. Open House, Sketchley Meadows Business Park, Hinckley, Leicestershire, LE10 3EY, U.K.

PaperDirect Pacific. 175 Briens Road, Unit Number 7, Northmead, NSW 2152, Australia.

Photography Stock Houses

When you want professional-quality photos, stock houses maintain an inventory of everything imaginable. You'll find them listed in the telephone directory.